Discovering
Self-Imagery

*weekly reflections to develop
a purposeful identity*

Discovering
Self-Imagery
weekly reflections to develop a purposeful identity

KILEY FLEMING, EdD

www.BookpressPublishing.com

Published in Des Moines, Iowa, by:

Bookpress Publishing
P.O. Box 71532
Des Moines, IA 50325
www.BookpressPublishing.com

Publisher's Cataloging-in-Publication Data

Names: Fleming, Kiley Anne, author.
Title: Discovering self-imagery : weekly reflections to develop a purposeful identity / Kiley Anne Fleming.
Description: Des Moines, IA: Bookpress Publishing, 2024.
Identifiers: LCCN: 2024909697 | ISBN: 978-1-947305-98-4
Subjects: LCSH Self-realization. | Self-actualization (Psychology). | Success. | Conduct of life. | Self-help. | Quality of life. | BISAC SELF-HELP / Personal Growth / Success | BODY, MIND & SPIRIT / Inspiration & Personal Growth | SELF-HELP / Communication & Social Skills
Classification: LCC BF637.S4 .F54 2024 | DDC 158.1--dc23

First Edition
Printed in the United States of America
10 9 8 7 6 5 4 3 2 1

CONTENTS

Discovering Self-Imagery 1

☐ _____ Week 1   **Remodeling** 5

☐ _____ Week 2   **Budgets** 9

☐ _____ Week 3   **Pacers** 13

☐ _____ Week 4   **Memes** 18

☐ _____ Week 5   **Badge of Honor** 22

☐ _____ Week 6   **Mowing** 28

☐ _____ Week 7   **Rubber Cement** 33

☐ _____ Week 8   **Stars** 37

☐ _____ Week 9   **Flawed** 41

☐ _____ Week 10   **Brown Noise** 45

☐ _____ Week 11   **Guarding** .49

☐ _____ Week 12   **Nail Polish** 53

☐ _____ Week 13   **Loss Leader** 57

☐ _____ Week 14   **New Hires** 61

☐ _____ Week 15   **Phone Crisis** 65

☐ _____ Week 16   **Fishing Lures** 69

☐ _____ Week 17   **Armageddon Pantry** 73

☐ _____ Week 18   **Titles** 77

☐ _____ Week 19   **Themes** 82

☐ _____ Week 20   **Typos** 86

☐ _____ Week 21   **Vault** 90

☐ _____ Week 22   **Track** 94

☐ _____ Week 23   **Party PREP** 98

☐ _____ Week 24   **Fifth Street** 102

☐ _____ Week 25   **Spring Break** 106

☐ _____ Week 26 Photographs 110

☐ _____ Week 27 Cookie Mystery 114

☐ _____ Week 28 Acronyms 118

☐ _____ Week 29 Brands 123

☐ _____ Week 30 Mirrors 127

☐ _____ Week 31 Ingredients 131

☐ _____ Week 32 Of Course 135

☐ _____ Week 33 Iron Sharpens Iron 139

☐ _____ Week 34 Embassies 143

☐ _____ Week 35 Oil Change 148

☐ _____ Week 36 Fonts 152

☐ _____ Week 37 License Plates 156

☐ _____ Week 38 Blazers 160

☐ _____ Week 39 Pivot 164

☐ _____ Week 40 And Also... 168

☐ _____ Week 41 Deposits and Withdrawals 172

☐ _____ Week 42 G.O.A.T. 176

☐ _____ Week 43 Leaves 181

☐ _____ Week 44 Sum 185

☐ _____ Week 45 Returning .189

☐ _____ Week 46 Diabetes and the Dance 193

☐ _____ Week 47 Safe Place .197

☐ _____ Week 48 Raw 201

☐ _____ Week 49 Fractures .205

☐ _____ Week 50 FOMO 210

☐ _____ Week 51 Air Quotes 215

☐ _____ Week 52 Three Words 219

Conclusion .223

Discovering Self-Imagery

People often believe that self-awareness should be innate because it ought to be natural to know ourselves better than anyone else on the planet. Because we can easily fall prey to the idea that we know ourselves well, it is easy to assume that understanding the relationships around us is where we need to first place our focus and efforts. Yet, interpersonal relationships, both the successes and pitfalls, often start with the foundation of the *intra*personal relationship. How well we know ourselves translates to external relational dynamics. This is where a holistic approach to imagery can lend a helping hand. When developed, a person's self-identified imagery can become a natural foundation for understanding oneself intrinsically since imagery relies on a reflective or mirroring practice. Once we begin using the tools of internal imagery methods, we can expand upon them in other facets of our lives.

Imagery is a way of connecting inner messages with cues shared universally among others, like symbols, metaphors, mantras, or pictures. The use of imagery creates shared understanding within relationships. Sometimes the very relationship needing the most attention is the one we have with ourselves. In the pursuit of discovering the imagery that connects our internal state to the external world, we create bridges. These bridges serve as platforms to the various realms that matter most to us individually: profession, friendship, neighborhood, romance, extracurricular, and family. All are well-served when the individuals involved in these relationships have connected their internal message with those external interactions that matter most to them. Imagery lays the groundwork for helping create the associations regarding our abstract internal state with concrete external concepts that are widely understood by those with whom we engage.

Having a set of tools to develop your imagery practice, much like learning any discipline in life, can create these guideposts. Whatever brings you to this workbook is intended to provide a framework for growth and development with your own intrapersonal understanding, which can then be used to advance the relationships around you. Not only will you value yourself more because you have direction about how you wish to shape your self-imagery through the process of evaluating the scope of your world, but you will have greater capacity to appreciate the self-imagery that others project toward you. This will enrich your ability to constructively problem-solve, interact effectively in difficult situations and with challenging individuals, and more fully enjoy the blessings of the relationships in which you chose to participate. Discovering self-identified imagery also helps with the achievement of goals, tasks, and objectives because there is a fundamental understanding of internally held functions, along with knowing what systems and individuals will augment those pursuits in a more successful manner.

The examples in this book are from my lived experience, and I appreciate that each reader has their own. Perspectives are highly unique to everyone, which is why we see different approaches and views taken by various individuals who, for all intents, are going through the same experience. Yet, no two people ever walk the exact same footprint. It is my hope that in sharing pieces of my world, you will reflect on your life and remember your own stories that shape who you are. Both the highlights and lowlights should be pondered when you consider what comprises your past. Nobody should be defined solely at either end of the spectrum because we are the sum of all that we have experienced, both rewarding and challenging. Discounting one or the other assigns our thoughts, energy, and focus to a narrow lens. Understandably, the memories and stories we use to inform our self-imagery tend to be either highly negative or positive, because the brain is designed to pay attention to extremes. Keep this in mind when you study what your mind recalls. Challenge yourself to think about the other end of the continuum and take time to deliberately assess areas that might seem ordinary or average. A lot of living happens between the extremes.

My stories are exactly that, my own. As a culture we spend a lot of time looking at the lives other people are living. It can produce all types of cognitive dissonance if we pay more attention to the narratives others give and fail to recognize our own along the way. Therefore, it may seem hypocritical for me to articulate my own stories when I am telling you there is a risk in focusing too much time and attention on the lives of others; however, this workbook is intended to create a weekly framework by which you can start your own journey of identifying the self-imagery that is meaningful to you. The questions at the end of each week's reading will help you see how I use life stories to develop concepts surrounding self-imagery. This methodology can become a mode for creating more tangible, significant, and efficient impressions that connect your internally held beliefs and values to your relationships, work, and pursuits. It removes a lot of the guesswork about why we behave in certain ways and why certain relationships manifest the way they do. Shared understanding charts a path. Join me in the process of developing self-imagery where you and I create our unique maps together.

WEEK

1

Remodeling

When I moved into my house, I recognized it was outdated com-
pared to the latest trends one might find on the market or while
watching the newest episodes on HGTV. As a newly divorced mom,
though, the space was functional for my kids and the location was
great. I jumped at the chance to buy a home while the market was
affordable. Within a year of living in the home, however, I began
feeling stifled in my very small kitchen. My children and I are not
small souls, so anytime the four of us would congregate, it felt like
a game of Tetris unfolding. I considered various solutions: knock
down walls, expand the footprint outside, update the original floor-
plan, or do nothing. I quickly assessed my values and decided that
doing nothing wouldn't make me happy but changing the layout was
cost prohibitive. I made the choice to work with the structure of the
small kitchen to maximize what was already there.

I studied this challenging kitchen for weeks. Upon reflection, I
discovered the dark color of the cabinets, the style of countertops,

and lack of lighting were causing the already small space to feel much smaller. With a bit of quick research, I realized I could paint the cabinets and countertops with products designed specifically for this function. While labor intensive and a bit backbreaking, it was very inexpensive and drastically changed the feel of the space. Having an electrician change lighting fixtures and installing new cabinet hardware both lightened the space and created better functionality.

The next step was creating a magnetic pegboard system to affix to the refrigerator. This allowed me to hang kitchen gadgets in an otherwise dead space while freeing up an entire drawer. I designed a rolling cart system to add more storage and prep space and hung pots and pans from the ceiling where the space was going to waste. Then I rounded out the project by painting the walls to add more style. With a few hundred dollars I created a space that is more suited to my creative vibe while increasing the functionality. It's still a small kitchen, but the cooking experience is now much more enjoyable for my family.

I could have spent a lot of time, money, and energy making the space bigger, but I decided to work with the history and blueprint of the kitchen. Sometimes a blank slate isn't a viable option and working creatively with what already exists makes more sense. The same can be true for us when we decide to work on self-improvement. A total reset, new template, or blank canvas might not be realistic. Instead, embracing some of the foundational footprints and history can encourage us to be creative problem-solvers, tenaciously resilient, or contented processors. Believing that the entirety of our past should be ignored or avoided can lead to a fixed mindset where we limit potential and opportunity. Conversely, thinking we are permanently bound by previous choices hedges our growth. Creative remodeling balances the concepts of form and function. Embracing who we are and infusing light and color into our perspective can enhance value and performance without gutting ourselves entirely.

 **Changepoints:**

Consider a place or space—whether in a home, event venue, or office/ business—where you creatively worked within the confines of what was already there:

■ How did it feel to use a different mindset to embrace an established setting instead of wiping the slate clean? How might this translate into your own personal development? _____

_____

_____

_____

■ Who in your life models an example of authentic self-acceptance while still seeking growth along the way? _____

_____

_____

■ What would the experience be like if you were more accepting of your history and background as you work on self-development? _____

_____

_____

_____

■ What areas in your life are you more prone to self-shame by trying to wish this part of your story away? _____

_____

_____

■ What positives can flow by embracing vulnerability and displaying this to others? _____

_____

_____

■ How might your journey be enhanced if you shifted to a mindset that balanced self-acceptance with self-improvement? _____

_____

_____

My kitchen is still small, but now it is a mighty space that serves my life well while still reflecting my values of being financially conscious, creative, and self-empowered.

Reflection:

_____
_____
_____
_____
_____
_____
_____
_____
_____
_____
_____
_____
_____
_____
_____
_____
_____
_____
_____
_____
_____
_____
_____
_____
_____

Budgets

When people think of budgets, it often brings to mind their financial constraints. The concept of a financial budget is to use funds within whatever means or goals the person set for him or herself. In many situations it is to avoid unwanted debt, although it can also be used as a tool to reach milestones. While many people think of a financial budget as a negative restriction, the purpose of a budget can also bring forth a lot of freedom through the disciplined process. People pay down their mortgages faster, enter retirement sooner, purchase luxury items, and embark on adventures through the process of financial budgeting.

By shifting the perspective to a positive lens, a monetary budget can be an empowering and educational resource. We know that if we need or want to spend less money than we make, thought should be given to reducing spending, absorbing debt, or establishing plans to earn more income. A budget doesn't have to be fixed and concrete as it can evolve with strategic efforts. The key is to act within self-determined factors that are motivating and achievable.

Applying these same principles, other areas in our lives could also benefit from the concept of budgeting. For instance, a health journey can be budgeted where food consumption and exercise are paired to determine the weight, energy, and wellness we wish to establish. Each one of us, just like a financial budget, has a unique set of contributors that determine our health factors, like metabolism and physical exercise thresholds. Together these can create a health budget to reduce issues, much like reducing financial debt, or improving areas similar to achieving financial benchmarks. Our BMI-weight scores, blood pressure, and physical flexibility are examples of long-game gauges on our short-term budgeting decisions surrounding our calorie intake, types of body movement through exercise, and genetic disposition.

Time and relationships can also be considered from the lens of a budget. The allotment of 24 hours in a day exists for everyone, and how that time is spent is something to assess. Sleep, work, parenting, recreation, exercise, and hobbies are just a few of the areas where time needs to be managed. Relationships, personalities, and temperaments, along with external demands on time or energy, can impact how we wish to budget interpersonal associations. We may wish to have a few quality relationships with selected individuals, whereas others use this budget to have many large social circles.

Knowing the criteria that impact each of our designated budgets helps us analyze gaps, create goals, and maintain the homeostasis we individually identify. No two people will have the same life budget, so our job isn't to determine how others should act in accordance with their established budget. Instead, our task is to self-reflect and intentionally behave in such a way that is consistent with the life budgets that mirror our unique internal values and beliefs. Then, we can rest easy knowing we are consuming or saving well within our own set life budgets.

Changepoints:

Think through a specific time where you wisely calculated your spending, nutrition, sleep, ability to juggle time, or relationship management:

■ How did this proper gauging affect you in other areas outside this specific parameter? _____

_____

_____

_____

■ How did this successful achievement benefit you and what long-term pitfalls did you avoid? _____

_____

_____

_____

● Who in your life has shown an ability to shift a budget in their life—health, time, money, relationships—where you could see growth or transformation?

_____

_____

_____

_____

■ How can this person serve as a mentor or guide as you select areas for improving your life budgets? _____

_____

_____

■ What are the detailed, specific benefits of achieving these goals? _____

_____

_____

_____

■ Who will reap the rewards of these efforts? _____

_____

_____

Living out our budgets is a way to shape our world in a manner that reflects our inner compass. They need not be viewed as a punitive, restrictive tool. Instead, they can be seen as a daily choice we are making to demonstrate a life that is regulated, empowered, and measured by our own mind and hands.

Reflection:

_____

_____

_____

_____

_____

_____

_____

_____

_____

_____

_____

_____

_____

_____

_____

_____

_____

_____

_____

_____

_____

WEEK
3

Pacers

Running has become a big part of my life after having three kids. Typically, when I join a race, I start the event with at least one person I know; however, at a particular half-marathon I ran, I didn't know anyone who had registered to participate. As a result, I thought it would be fun to search out a pacer to converse with at the beginning of the race. For those who aren't into the running scene, a pacer is someone who runs as a representative of the race by guaranteeing they will complete the race within a predetermined timeframe. As a side note, these athletes also run the entire time with a sign on a pole in their hand that states their pace…this is no easy feat, as I can barely chew gum and run at the same time. Therefore, if a participant runs an entire race with a pacer, they know they will finish the race within the goal time tethered to that pacer.

People run with pacers for a variety of reasons. Some runners tend to start races too fast, so pacers ensure they don't let their adrenaline get the best of them at the beginning. Other runners can suffer from mid-run bonks, so pacers help keep them sharp since neither the beginning nor the end is in sight. The pacer simply helps runners plow through that often-dreadful midsection. And, then there are some who struggle to finish the race. Pacers encourage them to complete what they started. Still others want to run with a pacer for simple companionship. Pacers are athletes who are very comfortable with running, know the racecourse well, and deliberately run the event slower than their true capability, which is how they guarantee their followers will get to the finish line within the goal time. These runners often talk to fellow runners the *entire* length of the race to motivate and encourage them (13.1 miles for half marathons and 26.2 miles for full marathons if you are doing the math!). For these reasons, they are great at meeting the various needs of the racers they are supporting.

In most circumstances in life we perform better, and more pleasantly, when we seek out a pacer to help us along the way. Whether our concern is starting out too fast, needing sustenance during the middle, encouragement to finish strong, or just simple conversation during the route, people are designed to be in fellowship with others. "Life pacers" can provide this fellowship because they are seasoned, know what to expect, how to help if things go awry, and don't get ruffled when thrown for a loop.

A pacer who aligns with your goals and helps you achieve an outcome can be used for a variety of reasons, like when:

- You are faced with a new circumstance or task.

- You are unsure of your ability in an area.

- You anticipate you might need support at some midpoint during an undertaking.

- You feel isolated or discouraged.

- You simply want to enrich an experience.

You may not be a literal runner. That is okay. But remember that life—in all forms—is a race. Why not be more effective, efficient, and encouraged with the presence of a pacer? All areas of life benefit from finding a safe person to be a life pacer.

Changepoints:

Think through your personal history and consider a future area when you might actively seek a "pacer":

■ When do you lose motivation or progress along the way? _____

_____

_____

_____

■ What are the areas where you already shine and would feel elation if you went to the next level? _____

_____

_____

_____

■ Where can you anticipate you might need support at some point during a specific undertaking to achieve an outcome? What does that assistance look like? _____

_____

_____

_____

■ When might you benefit from the aid of someone wiser and more experienced than yourself? _____

_____

_____

_____

■ What is something you simply want to enrich even though there is nothing inherently wrong? How would it feel to pursue this? _____

_____

_____

_____

■ Who are the identified pacers in your life? _____

_____

_____

Find a pacer. Run a good race.

Reflection:

_____
_____
_____
_____
_____
_____
_____
_____
_____
_____
_____
_____
_____
_____
_____
_____
_____
_____
_____
_____
_____
_____
_____
_____
_____
_____

WEEK
4

Memes

Memes can be a creative communication tool. These simple pictures pack a powerful punch because they deliver a message with such clarity. My coworker is the queen of memes and will send the best images to match the situation we are facing. Usually, she addresses a challenging situation with memes that create much needed gut-laughter. It instantly diffuses the unpleasantries by shedding light in comical ways. Often it is just a picture. If any words are used, they are few.

These little icons are highly effective because they rely on imagination, shared understanding, and brevity. Next time you pick up your phone, look around at the world of memes and find out just how many exist. And therein lies the rub: finding the right meme. Sometimes it takes searching many phrases until the right imagery pops up. To make the meme work, however, requires that it conveys an accurate message. Therefore, rarely will the sender just use a random meme. Art and science were used to find the perfect image.

When communicating something that could evoke stress, misunderstanding, or tension, consider the process of developing a meme. Memes work because they first think about the topic at hand and then winnow it down to an image that captures the concept. They also work because the recipient is in mind when capturing the icon. Lastly, it rests on the philosophy of simplicity and directness to communicate. By using a shared understanding of the topic being conveyed, the meme gets right to the point with imagination and succinctness. And, usually, it breathes oxygen into an otherwise weighty conversation.

This isn't to say all communication woes in the world can be dealt with through memes, but the mindset can often be applied in a universal way. There are enough critics, downers, and sharp-tongued people in the world already. We don't need to add to this equation. Instead, think like a meme and see how the conversation unfolds.

Changepoints:

Using a smartphone, go to a meme setting and scroll through images:

■ Which images resonate with you? What about their composition strikes a chord? Is it the color usage, picture choice, or brief word selection that you appreciate? _____

_____

_____

_____

■ Consider a time when a meme was sent to you, and it was highly effective. How did it change your mindset? How did communication alter? _____

_____

_____

_____

_____

■ In what ways could you adopt the philosophies that make memes so successful? _____

_____

_____

_____

■ What parts of your world could benefit from the metaphoric use of memes?

_____

_____

_____

_____

■ Who are the people who would appreciate it? _____

_____

_____

■ How might those relationships change? _____

_____

_____

If it seems obvious to use a meme-mindset to deal with challenges, just embrace the well-known meme and say, "Thanks Captain Obvious."

Reflection:

WEEK
5

Badge of Honor

When does a person's career pursuit move from being inspired and passionate to residing in the world of workaholism? Furthermore, why do we often applaud workaholism as a badge of honor?

I was speaking with a friend who was a fresh medical school graduate beginning the grueling residency process. When I asked what his schedule was like, he told me the maximum time the hospital has them work is 80 hours per week and a minimum of 60 hours per week. Baffled by this overwhelming workload, I sought the perspective of another person who explained that we should all want residents to work so much to ensure exposure to as many medical situations as possible during their three-year residency. While this is a logical argument, I can't help but wonder if this structure is the best for these doctors or patients who receive their care. After all, if a doctor works 80 hours in a six-day work week, they are essentially working over 13 hours per day. This only leaves them 11 remaining hours to recharge their batteries in an environment outside the medical facility. If a doctor is approaching 13 hours on their shift, who would want to be the patient receiving this care? Yet, on the flip side, I am forever indebted to the labor and delivery nurse who worked past the end of her shift to ensure my first-born son entered the world safely. Kudos to her for the passion and dedication to medicine. I give this example because I know nothing is ever all good or all bad. After all, inspired employees are the backbone of thriving companies. This is certainly not a forum to encourage laziness.

What happens, however, when inspiration goes down the slippery workaholism slope? Does workaholism even have to be found in the number of hours the person works? What about the person who works a "regular" schedule but cannot mentally let it go when they leave their employer? Perhaps they aren't as engaged in their normal life because the preoccupation with work prevents them from fully engaging in the present moment. This would describe me in my former work life. While I worked a part-time schedule, I found myself constantly torn by the requirements of my job while I was at home. I would field emails and phone calls during my days "off." I wore this as a badge of honor. I was needed. I was helping the lives of the employees at my company. I was a champion for justice, right? But, what about the justice that my home-life was seeking from me? Why wasn't it enough for me to be present right at home with my three little ones? Therefore, even with an ideal part-time, flexible work schedule, I made the decision to quit this job and dive into full-time mommyhood for a season. I am not advocating that women need to be at home to avoid workaholism, although I am a living example that workaholism can take many shapes and sizes. It can exist outside of the typical full-time corporate world, because workaholism is sneaky like that. It will sneak up on any unsuspecting soul who doesn't have enough guardrails in place. So, let's pause to consider if these scenarios might be workaholism:

…The truck driver who is technically driving under the government hour requirements, and therefore dismisses the danger of taking energy drinks when driving on the road while sleepy and tired.

…The pastor who attends every congregation visit so as not to tax the church members to find more volunteers, while the pastor's spouse quietly attends to the needs within their own home.

…The principal of a school who attends every single school function because the students and parents absolutely must see her presence, even though her own children would love to have more time learning under her care.

…The police officer who signs up for as many overtime shifts as possible to help protect and serve, while he secretly drowns in his own depression because his personal time to engage in social outlets is limited.

…The retail manager who works every holiday shift to give his staff a break, but never sees his own parents or siblings on the holidays.

This isn't intended to shame anyone or send anyone on a guilt trip. Rather, it is to acknowledge that workaholism is a real issue, and it isn't just relegated to the CEO of a company. When we revere people for living on four hours of sleep for pursuing work goals or praise professionals for climbing the corporate ladder at the detriment of their outside lives, we perpetuate the cycle. We encourage the myth that this is admirable and maintainable without costs in other areas of life. Perhaps we should be more careful about what badges of honor we choose to wear and which we choose to award other people. Props to those who have found a way to balance the delicate pendulum of working diligently and embracing the other facets of life. This is a true badge of honor.

Changepoints:

You might knowingly or unknowingly engage in workaholism when you measure:

■ Where do you continually feel a heavy professional stressor that you can't seem to create peace within? _____

_____

_____

_____

_____

■ In what areas are you driven by money or prestige more than you care to admit? _____

_____

_____

_____

_____

■ Are there times where you are more comfortable with your work life than any of your other identities? _____

_____

_____

_____

_____

■ How can you establish healthy boundaries to protect yourself from moving from passion to pitfall? _____

_____

_____

_____

■ Which people in your life can act as a support system or referee when you are placing too much emphasis on your work? _____

_____

_____

_____

_____

Be a great worker, but also be a greater achiever of life.

Reflection:

_____

_____

_____

_____

_____

_____

_____

_____

_____

_____

_____

_____

_____

_____

_____

_____

_____

_____

_____

_____

_____

_____

_____

_____

_____

_____

_____

_____

_____

_____

_____

Mowing

Using a lawnmower wasn't a skill I possessed until my late thirties. Admittedly, I dodged this task by virtue of having a dad who enjoyed the outdoors and liked mowing. Later, my brothers assumed this task and eventually I married a man who was meticulous in the lawn care department. To reveal the depth of my ineptness, I will share about the first time I was asked to mow. My father-in-law, at the time, asked me to start the mower. Eager to help, I went to the garage to rev up the engine; however, there was no "ON" button for me to push. I searched and fumbled around, but alas I was defeated. I came back inside and told him about my lack of success. Being a wonderful human being, he simply smiled and chuckled. He assured me that it was okay and took care of it. Missing my opportunity to learn from a pro, I went about my merry way. Only years later when I purchased my own lawnmower did I realize what a dolt he must have thought he inherited for a daughter-in-law. It was a good lesson in the power of allowing a naïve gal to save face.

Fast forward to my late thirties when I was newly single and needed to manicure the lawn. I went to the local hardware store and trapped an unsuspecting salesperson. He didn't know what he was stumbling upon when he decided to help me purchase this grass-trimming beast. But he quickly assessed that I had no clue what I was doing, which was given away when he said, "You really have *NEVER* mowed a lawn before?!" Thankfully, he took this as a challenge and decided I was his newfound project. He took me everywhere in the store to teach me about the oil it uses, where to fill the gas, how to tell when the blades need sharpening, and basically how to avoid losing any digits in the process of cutting the grass. It was at this store where I also learned lawnmowers are started with a pull-chord and not a magic button that I was previously searching for when my father-in-law made his request of me. This salesman was a good soul. He spent far more time and energy than I expected to find at a hardware store.

When we ended our adventure together, he said, "If you were my daughter, I'd tell to enjoy the process of mowing the lawn." Apparently, my doubtful look gave me away, because then he said, "It's one of the few beautiful things in life where you instantly get to see the benefit of your handiwork. Take this approach and I promise you'll feel differently about mowing your lawn."

To my shock, he was right. Every pass I made across my lawn was proof of my effort. As I went along, I noticed that the smell of the grass was amazing. The sun was energizing, and I was getting extra steps in for the day. After I finished the task, I decided to think about other areas where the same principle applies, like folding laundry and shoveling snow. With laundry, the smell of clean clothes and seeing the neatly folded piles is rewarding. With shoveling, the fresh air and soaking in the pure white of new snow is incredible.

These are only a few examples, but the lesson can be expanded upon. When we take tasks and decide to look for areas of incremental completion and the gifts given along the way, it changes how it feels to embark upon it. If there is a book to read, chunk the assignment into chapters. If there is a report that is due, break it down into palatable sections. Create to-do lists for the mental sake of feeling the euphoria of checking things off. Even simply making the bed in the morning can set a positive tone for the entire day.

And in the process of tackling a new task, you might just learn something cool, like the fact that a lawnmower starts by using a bit of brute strength, powered with the ingenuity of physics.

Changepoints:

Consider the steps of mowing the lawn, folding laundry, or shoveling snow:

■ What similar steps could be applied in your personal or professional life?

_____

_____

_____

_____

■ How would an incremental approach change the way you view tasks in your life that you would rather avoid? _____

_____

_____

_____

■ Who do you have in your inner circle who would be able to help you set goals and the steps required to complete them? _____

_____

_____

_____

■ What are the first tasks you can set about accomplishing? _____

_____

_____

_____

_____

■ How does seeing tangible completion of a step create motivation for the next step? _____

_____

_____

■ How could achievement of these tasks lead to bigger dreams? _____

_____

_____

_____

Like mowing a lawn, achieving most goals is accomplished one step, one pass, one row at a time.

Reflection:

_____

_____

_____

_____

_____

_____

_____

_____

_____

_____

_____

_____

_____

_____

_____

_____

_____

_____

_____

_____

_____

_____

_____

_____

_____

_____

_____

_____

WEEK

7

Rubber Cement

There was an extensive period in my life that was extremely difficult for a variety of reasons. As I reflect on the journey, I have come to understand more about how I dealt with the circumstances thrust upon me and those I created by my own series of choices. Rubber cement is a good way of describing this timeframe. Remember rubber cement from elementary school? Opening the metal canister would fill the room with a noxious smell not easy to clear from the sinuses. When we affixed the soon-to-be masterpieces in front of us the glue would inevitably stick to our hands and make a goopy mess. The magic of rubber cement, however, is that when it dries you can rub your fingers and the glue becomes a rubber-like ball which easily falls off the hands and the smell disappears. Incredible stuff, rubber cement is.

Rubber cement works two ways. If the glue is placed on just one surface, it creates a flexible, nonpermanent bond that can be repositioned later; however, if the glue is placed on both surfaces and then allowed to dry first, it becomes a permanent bond when placed together. It's a magical process if you can tolerate the initial stink and messiness. Isn't that life as well? Sometimes you must tolerate the smell and stickiness before the masterpiece unfolds. You also must decide how you are going to approach the glue. Is a permanent bond needed or is something flexible desired?

For the longest time, I kept trying to make the wrong types of bonds work without understanding the true nature of the glue. It's only successful when both sides are involved in the right way. My controlling nature continually tried to work against the chemistry of rubber cement. For instance, I exhausted myself trying a flexible approach when that wasn't in the best interest of the project. Conversely, I also exhausted myself by forcing permanency when this was destroying the artwork that was intended to unfold. Eventually, I became altogether afraid to open the rubber cement canister, because I wasn't confident I could handle the smell or the mess. As a result, I wasn't mindful of how to approach what was in front of me. Instead, I attempted to glue things together in a haphazard way. Admittedly, I made a disaster of my world in areas like failing to address my crumbling marriage, isolating from friendships, and keeping family at a distance.

Then, I took a deep breath and realized the stench wouldn't last forever if I decided to finally use the glue the right way. I started studying the projects in front of me and began using the rubber cement more productively. My children, my work, my doctoral studies, and meaningful relationships became my purpose to thrive. Something wonderful resulted: the masterpieces already in my reach became my joy. True joy. I let the glue work the way it was intended. Any glue that stuck to my hand wasn't going to stay there forever. If I let it dry, I could now rub it off. The smell disappeared, and something beautiful revealed itself.

Changepoints:

As you begin to open your "rubber cement" canister to create a new work of art, ponder:

■ How will you allow yourself to cope with the smell and mess of gluing your life together while you tackle what is ahead? _____

_____

_____

_____

_____

■ What strategies will you use to approach what needs to be glued in your life with the best perspective? _____

_____

_____

_____

_____

■ What will you look for to decide if what you are facing needs a permanent or flexible tactic? _____

_____

_____

_____

_____

■ How will you know when the glue has dried enough to touch the masterpiece in front of you? _____

_____

_____

_____

_____

■ Are you willing to remove the unneeded glue from your fingers that doesn't serve in your best interest or the finished project? _____

_____

_____

_____

_____

Embrace the process of allowing rubber cement in your life. Glue it, rub your fingers to get rid of the extra glue when you are done, breathe in the now clean air, and soak in the resulting beauty.

Reflection:

_____

_____

_____

_____

_____

_____

_____

_____

_____

_____

_____

_____

_____

_____

_____

_____

_____

_____

_____

_____

_____

_____

_____

_____

_____

WEEK

8

Stars

"Star treatment." "Shine like a star." "Star student." "Be a star." "Hollywood star." These are phrases we associate with exceptional, high-performing people. We correlate the attributes of stars hanging in the night sky with amazing brilliance. This is a fair assessment since these celestial lights stand in stark contrast to the blackness of the evening sky.

Most of us learned in science class that stars are burning masses located light years away, and the closest is the sun. There are lesser-known facts, however, about the 200-400 billion stars in the sky that have lessons to teach. The next time you look at these constellations or praise someone for having star qualities, remember the pieces of information that often don't come readily to mind. For instance, when we see stars twinkle, it isn't because the star is doing something out of the ordinary; rather, it is the movement in the earth's atmosphere that creates this fun sparkle. It's the quiet work of the atmosphere that lays the backdrop for the star to get credit. Also, stars with the most mass are the ones that live the shortest period. The requirement to produce so much energy shortens their lifespan. Having a great amount of mass comes at the cost of burning faster. Sometimes a steadier, understated presence can have its own reward of a longer existence.

The next nugget of wisdom to consider about stars is profound: stars are in perfect balance, yet stars are in continual conflict with themselves. There is a gravitational pull of their mass that is constantly pulling them inward. Left unchecked, stars would merely collapse. This doesn't happen, however, because there is a force that pushes back: light! The core of a star produces enough energy to balance the gravitational pull. The result is the illumination we see at night. This is remarkable given how far away stars are from earth and yet, we can see their beauty with the naked eye.

It makes sense why we use the analogy of a star to characterize greatness. The physical brilliance is noteworthy. Yet, the symbolic brilliance is equally remarkable. It is also the subtle working of the atmosphere that creates the glimmer we admire. Perhaps this is the extremely important role you take in the world. Also, it is the star with lesser mass that lasts the longest. Maybe you, too, take this steadfast approach to life. Regardless of the role we take in the universe, it is important to remember that stars shine not because it is effortless. The harmony of the light comes because the internal core of the star works in balance against gravity by using its own source of energy. Each of us has this ability within, so we are all tasked with the responsibility of shining in the environment we've been given. Let us all be our own star.

Changepoints:

*Next time you look up at the night sky and
see stars, pause to observe them, and consider:*

■ Upon looking at stars, what human attributes come to mind? Are you currently modeling these traits? _____

_____

_____

_____

■ Think of a specific time when you felt positive about yourself. What behaviors did you engage in to get to this point? _____

_____

_____

_____

■ Are there potential shifts in your atmosphere that will help produce a needed glimmer of self-encouragement? How can you foster your internal core to produce energy to make a difference in your world? _____

_____

_____

_____

■ How can you create inner balance to ensure you don't burn out quickly?

_____

_____

_____

■ What inspires you to stay engaged for the long run? _____

_____

_____

_____

■ How has the world around you benefited from this approach? _____

_____

_____

_____

Balance in life comes from an acknowledgement that life has a gravitational pull, and we have the internal power to create light that works with it. This is how we glow.

Reflection:

_____

_____

_____

_____

_____

_____

_____

_____

_____

_____

_____

_____

_____

_____

_____

_____

_____

_____

_____

_____

_____

_____

_____

_____

_____

_____

WEEK
9

Flawed

Someone influential in my life described themselves as being flawed. I don't consider this person to be flawed because I feel they are incredible. The concept of being flawed, however, has resonated with me since I heard the person use it to describe a personality attribute. When I looked up the word, I discovered that it means, "a feature that mars the perfection of something." After reading this definition, I decided that I would absolutely prefer to spend my time around authentically flawed individuals than pseudo perfect ones. Have you ever listened to a captivating musician or viewed the works of a wonderful artist and realized their talent resides in embracing imperfections? I like a little bit of messiness in my world. It's more interesting. It's more palatable. It's more inspiring.

Anyone who knows me will attest to the fact that I am peppered with imperfections. I'm frequently impatient. My responses often outweigh the circumstances at hand. I can have an assertive tongue. My expectations of others can be out of line. I typically move at hyper-speed. Flawed, I certainly am. I spent years inwardly apologizing away my personality as being less than acceptable, because it wasn't the picture of perfection. Recently, I have been challenged—by the same person who said he was flawed—to consider a lens of love when looking at the world. The flaws in the universe make it beautiful, creative, and remarkable. Many "mistakes" have led to amazing discoveries. Did you know the creation of the chocolate chip cookie initially came about as the result of a flaw? Ruth Wakefield, owner of the Toll House Inn, had to adapt a recipe and broke up pieces of sweetened chocolate to replace baker's chocolate. She thought the chocolate "chips" would melt together, but instead the future of the chocolate chip cookie was created. I, for one, would love to hug Ruth for embracing a perceived flaw and creating one of my favorite desserts.

Creativity is where flaws are often beautified. Modigliani is one of my favorite artists, and I would encourage you to study his works if you haven't done so already. I love his works of women because he had a fascinating ability to distort the images into something wonderful. A perfect portrait wasn't his aim. He sought to show the world a different way of looking at the human body. And in the fashion industry, you might notice that articles of clothing now have tags on them that let people know they may find intentional flaws in the fabric. It's purposeful because who wants to always be surrounded by the myth of perfection? Originality often flows from externally perceived mistakes.

I am so grateful I was introduced to the concept of flaws. More importantly, I am glad I was challenged to embrace self-flaws and people-flaws with a spirit of love and humility. After all, we are all works of art that are still being masterfully and interestingly created. And I shall happily ponder this concept while eating a perfectly imperfect chocolate chip cookie.

Changepoints:

Encourage yourself to embrace your "flaws" by asking:

■ When are you most likely to be too harsh on yourself or others? What areas that you perceive to be flawed could lead to something special? _____

_____

_____

_____

■ Who do you surround yourself with who encourages self-discovery, even if it means you might fall or make mistakes? _____

_____

_____

■ What are the areas in your life or activities you don't explore because you are afraid of not being perfect or needing to instantly be the best? _____

_____

_____

_____

■ What messages do you send yourself about striving for perfection? Are they rooted in a necessary reality or are you being overly critical? _____

_____

_____

■ Are there activities or interests you might consider if you weren't concerned about failing or afraid of the critical opinions of others? _____

_____

_____

■ What is preventing you from swinging for the fences? _____

_____

_____

■ What actions can you take to assess your threshold for flawed living?

_____

_____

Be courageously, wonderfully, and beautifully flawed!

Reflection:

_____
_____
_____
_____
_____
_____
_____
_____
_____
_____
_____
_____
_____
_____
_____
_____
_____
_____
_____
_____
_____
_____
_____
_____
_____
_____
_____
_____
_____

WEEK
10

Brown Noise

While attempting to get my household technology to produce background noise to assist with sleep, I verbally told the device to play "white noise." When my kids heard me instructing it to create this specific type of sound, they asked why that was the choice I selected. I must have looked baffled because they proceeded to shed light on my ignorance surrounding the topic. There are lots of "colored" noises, I was soon enlightened. Conversation among the family unfolded about why each person liked a particular noise color. I proceeded to scroll through a list of options and found that I prefer brown noise. Here I naively thought white noise was the only choice.

During this investigative process, I discovered sound engineers initially name the noise frequency to the color which loosely captures the light frequency that would correlate if the sound were a color. The first sound that was defined this way was white noise, hence why it is the one most referred to when people seek soothing background noise.

I have since discovered at least 11 sound colors, some technical and others informal. All seek to depict the relationship between the sound wave output and the light color frequency. Pink, green, and blue noise are just three of the colored noises to which a person can sleep or meditate. Interestingly, brown noise is named after Brownian Motion and is also known by the name "random walk" noise. It seems like a fitting name for how I often live my life, so perhaps this is why it resonates with me as I sleep.

Our words are also sounds, and they carry vibrations and light. Whether it is a positive, bright light largely rests upon us. We can't necessarily control how our words are received, but to a high degree we can use intention to shape our words in such a way that the energy, speed, and frequency spread the message in the way we desire, both to help or to harm.

Next time we speak, let's truly pause to contemplate the words and the intended vibrations to help us with the delivery. If we wish for our language to carry positivity, we must study the energy we are infusing with it. Sound and light go together. We can decide if we want to be violet light or noisy black light. If we prefer to shine through our communication, it starts with a partnership between the literal words and energy behind them.

Changepoints:

Play through the list of available background noise colors and listen to the nuances of the options:

■ How do the differences among the background noise choices translate to the way you think about communication in your own life? _____

_____

_____

_____

■ How can you shift the way you hear others to capture the vibration they intend to convey? _____

_____

_____

_____

■ Who in your life demonstrates the ability to balance their words, beliefs, and energy together? _____

_____

_____

_____

■ What facets of your life could be improved by paying attention to the energy you place into your communication? _____

_____

_____

_____

■ What relationships or tasks will be augmented by doing so? _____

_____

_____

_____

■ How will you chart a path to match your "noise" with your "light"? _____

_____

_____

_____

Color is a beautiful way to capture the spectrum between intent and impact as it pertains to the bridging of our noise and our light. May our energy authentically align with the image we hold out to the universe.

Reflection:

_____

_____

_____

_____

_____

_____

_____

_____

_____

_____

_____

_____

_____

_____

_____

_____

_____

_____

_____

_____

_____

_____

_____

_____

_____

_____

_____

_____

WEEK
11

Guarding

My massage therapist told me my muscles were so guarded that the individual muscles felt like they were lumped together as one large muscle. She said she was unable to work between the individual muscles, because my muscle guarding was so severe. I have always known I am a person who struggles to relax, but I didn't realize it was an issue at a physical level within my body. With the feedback from the massage therapist in mind, I decided to research muscle guarding. And, sure enough, it isn't a myth.

Muscle guarding is the nervous system's attempt at protecting the body from a perceived threat. Often, it occurs as a direct response to bodily injury…but for some, the root source of the stressor doesn't appear as obviously. Whether the bodily stress is real or perceived, the muscles respond by attempting to guard the body from harm. In short doses, muscle guarding can be a beneficial, protective measure for the body. Chronic, sustained muscle guarding, however, is counterproductive as it creates more issues than it remedies.

What if we applied the concepts of muscle guarding to the way we live our lives? In appropriate doses, guarding can be a useful response to hurtful or injury-prone situations; however, a constant state of tension can be damaging. In fact, when the body guards a certain area for prolonged periods, it often starts fatiguing and damaging other areas of the body that aren't in any danger of threat. In my personal life, if I decide to be selective and acute with my use of guarding, this can serve me well. But, if I allow my guarding to be long-lived and not discerning, I put myself at serious risk for strain, weariness, and unease.

Research reveals that two components need to exist to help people with muscle guarding: 1. Identify if there is a root cause and 2. Create a safe atmosphere that encourages authentic relaxation. Most experts agree that it is a gradual process of retraining the body to relax and trust again. Surely the same principles can be applied in our personal lives. If we feel we are chronically guarded, perhaps we could benefit from reflecting on potential causes of the guarding and from finding environments and relationships that foster true release. Then, give grace to allow the journey to be a steady progression toward relaxed acceptance.

If you are seeking to reduce guarding in your life, consider a variety of avenues that fit you. Slowly share pieces of your life that don't feel personally threatened with people you can be real with, until you are able to naturally share more freely. Evaluate what past sources have caused you stress or distrust and determine if there are measures you can take to release these from your life. Find people who appreciate you for who you are and who will genuinely be overjoyed to get to know you at your core.

Changepoints:

You may knowingly or unknowingly suffer from "life guarding" that is revealed during the process of awakening your spirit's muscles:

■ What do your external behaviors tell you about your internal thoughts?

_____

_____

_____

_____

_____

■ What environments cause you to struggle to be transparent with people in your life, even people who you are supposed to be close to? _____

_____

_____

_____

_____

■ In what ways are you afraid to let down walls due to past hurts? _____

_____

_____

_____

_____

■ When do you deflect if you are asked questions to distract people from getting to know you on a deeper level? _____

_____

_____

_____

■ What circumstances stir an initial reaction of defensiveness if something happens to you, instead of naturally providing the benefit of the doubt?

_____

_____

_____

Relax. Self-accept. Seek transparency. Allow the muscles of your soul to become unguarded.

Reflection:

WEEK

12

Nail Polish

The use of nail polish is typically seen as a way of beautifying one's hands. The styles and colors adorning many fingernails are admired by people across the world. Often painted to match outfits, seasons, and holidays, decorated nails are a trend universally appreciated by aesthetically driven folks. It is an outward symbol of an internal value as it takes time, effort, and money to keep up groomed hands, even those that aren't professionally maintained but are kept up at home.

Beyond prettiness, another benefit of manicures is that nail polish reduces the likelihood of getting chipped, broken, or snagged fingernails. It acts as a buffer from elements that otherwise weaken the nail. Some people can't grow long fingernails without the aid of nail polish, and I am one of those unfortunate souls. That's why polish plays an important part of a grooming regimen, even if it is just clear in color.

Because my natural nails are tragic at best, I was intrigued by the gel nail polish trend. It requires an LED lamp to set the specialized nail polish to the fingernail. What results is a longer lasting and more durable paint. As someone who previously couldn't grow their fingernails, this has been an astonishing and fun discovery. The UV light essentially cures the paint and provides my nails with strength not found alone.

Nail polish reflects a lot about how life can work. Sometimes a clear coat is what is needed to provide a transparent and thinner buffer. Nail polish also acts as a method of highlighting what is naturally there. Other times, colored paint helps augment the mood, message, or tone. Still other times, gel polish that is cured, strengthened, and set through light helps deliver the best results. It might all fall under the category of nail polish, but the form and function vary considerably. Light, color, and transparency all help at different points with the message and strength of what lies beneath. It is remarkable how one resource can provide a variety of benefits. Maybe we need to be nail polish to someone in our life, or maybe we need to receive the gift of nail polish. It can take what is already there and augment it to what it wouldn't be on its own.

Changepoints:

Look around you and see the varying types of nail polishes around you:

■ What subtle and bold messages are conveyed by what you see? _____
_____
_____
_____

■ How does nail polish act to improve the fingernail and in what ways could this be translated into your own life? _____
_____
_____
_____

■ What assumptions do you make about the fingernails you see around you, both good and bad? Where do these assumptions stem from and how can you learn from these thoughts? _____
_____
_____
_____

■ In what ways can you act as polish, or a support, to those around you?
_____
_____
_____
_____

■ What areas in your life could use a transparent coat to boost what is naturally there? _____
_____
_____

■ How can you work on strengthening what you already are at your core?
_____
_____
_____

Nail polish is a simple metaphor that can be used to teach us how to look at the mundane in a new way, and how to bolster what we might take for granted on its own. We just might have the ability to be the light, strength, and transparency for the world around us.

Reflection:

_____

_____

_____

_____

_____

_____

_____

_____

_____

_____

_____

_____

_____

_____

_____

_____

_____

_____

_____

_____

_____

_____

_____

_____

_____

WEEK
13

Loss Leader

Any title that has the word "loss" in it might resonate as negative. "Loss leader," however, is an intentional decision to do something at a cost with the long-term result of reaping a gain. Some companies sell a specific product at a deficit to get people through their doors, whereby hopefully increasing additional sales with other products. Other organizations give away products to create marketing connections. Where I am employed, we have chip-clips, lip balms, stress balls, pens, and notepads with the logo affixed on each item. There is never the assumption the recipient would pay a dime for these products. We shoulder the cost with the aim of increasing brand recognition. Therefore, these pieces of swag serve as a loss leader because we use the upfront sacrifice to create paths for greater things in the future.

Look around and you will see this approach is often taken using reduced-price products, coupons or discounts, and free items. The idea of these things being loss leaders doesn't drum up a negative connotation to those deciding to supply them. The managers and sales staff do it willingly because their perspective is shaped toward long-term relationships and business cultivation through an upfront decision to sacrifice for enduring connections.

Wouldn't it be a shift in our personal lives if we decided to purposefully make initial sacrifices for the sake of longer, more significant goals? Perhaps not eating that extra piece of birthday cake because bathing suit season is approaching in several months. Or paying the important bills before dipping into the checkbook to go on a shopping spree so there isn't stress at the end of the month. Or turning off the television before the show ends for the sake of grabbing a few more minutes of needed shut eye due to an important morning meeting.

Let's take it a bit deeper. Like deciding to offer an apology even if we feel our accountability to the situation is less than the other person so that an enduring relationship can be maintained. Or volunteering to work longer hours when we'd rather be doing something else to help an overwhelmed coworker so that the working environment remains relaxed. Maybe lending a neighbor a tool they need, even though you aren't sure it will be returned in pristine condition, because the collective upkeep of the community matters.

Keeping tallies is a recipe for feeling disadvantaged because the scope is fixed on the immediate. Instead, remember that a temporary or short-term loss can be eternally impactful. By deciding where to focus our energy—in long-term dividends—we enhance the quality of life, not only of those around us, but we, ourselves, benefit from all that flows as well. The loss leader becomes a living model for others to see. It helps in goal achievement, buoying relationships, and value enhancement. Whether it is to meet a weight-loss objective, save for a vacation, or enrich the lives we are surrounded by, demonstrating a loss leader approach serves to make the world a more meaningful, productive, and wonderful place.

Changepoints:

*Consider a time where you made a choice
to intentionally set short-term gains aside
to reach a long-term plan:*

■ How did the process of deciding to sacrifice feel initially and then how did it evolve down the line? _____

_____

_____

_____

■ Who were the people in your life who knew about your plan to make a deliberate sacrifice for the greater good? _____

_____

_____

_____

■ If there was push-back in creating this boundary, how did you address or remedy it? _____

_____

_____

_____

■ What are specific areas where the loss leader perspective could now be applied to your life? _____

_____

_____

_____

■ What changes in behaviors are required to plan for success? _____

_____

_____

■ How will you and others benefit from decisions that might initially appear challenging or sacrificing? _____

_____

_____

Each one of us has the capacity to become a leader in our respective worlds by choosing things that might appear to have an outside cost. Instead of feeling diminished, think like a person who generously gives out swag into the universe for the sake of infusing good energy. Your logo, or legacy, will be branded every time you do so.

Reflection:

_____
_____
_____
_____
_____
_____
_____
_____
_____
_____
_____
_____
_____
_____
_____
_____
_____
_____
_____
_____
_____
_____
_____
_____
_____
_____
_____

WEEK
14

New Hires

When you hire new employees after years of having tenured staff, you quickly recognize all the things you previously said or acted upon where you didn't give much contemplation due to the similar footing everyone shared. Things like work attire, schedules, acronyms, and processes take on new meaning to a novice entering a company. Hiring staff is an opportunity to reflect upon former ways of doing things while bringing newness into the fold. Making assumptions is a recipe for confusion and chaos if you aren't deliberate in your approach as the manager.

Even if you aren't a supervisor in an organizational sense, we all manage areas of our lives: our homes, social endeavors, work capacity, etc. When we get overly comfortable in those settings it is easy to assume that everyone is on the same page. It's understandable to falsely believe that everyone involved speaks the same language, holds the same shared values, and has the same beliefs.

For example, I was rambling on about something to my kids and they informed me that my words made no sense to them. We got a kick out of the fact that I was so tired I was conveying instructions in an utterly incoherent fashion. I truly believe I was speaking "mom-hasn't-slept" gibberish. What if this conversation had unfolded, however, when we were under stress, if it was regarding something very important, or if it was a novel concept they were seeking to understand? I doubt we would have found the humor then.

If we transfer the freshness of a new hire/management perspective to routine things we do in life, I am confident we would provide more clarity and dialogue to those who need it. It's easy to slip into autopilot without remembering that many times people benefit from more direction and insight. Additionally, it's simple to forget that people need compassion and understanding in areas we take for granted. We were all novices at one point, so a shift in viewpoints can help everyone navigate life with less tumult. When we interact by changing our pace, providing different types of information, or opening our emotional bandwidth, others get the opportunity to grow quicker and with fewer errors. This, in turn, should help reduce our level of frustration as well. So, it's a win-win when we pivot. The newbie isn't the only beneficiary of our change because authentic living is about continually evaluating the handbook of life.

Changepoints:

Remember when you started a new occupation and recall what was effective or ineffective in your onboarding:

■ How would you define a good supervisor-subordinate relationship in the broader sense of just employment? _____

_____

_____

_____

■ What does it look like from your lens to effectively make something approachable or digestible for the sake of in-depth learning? _____

_____

_____

_____

■ In what areas of your life could you provide more detailed feedback, transparent interactions, or benefit-of-the-doubt to those less seasoned than yourself?

_____

_____

_____

■ How will you ensure that you instill patience as you allow others, and yourself, to grow? _____

_____

_____

■ Who models these virtues in your life so that you can replicate similarities?

_____

_____

_____

■ How will you create checks-and-balances for yourself to prevent the habit of slipping into autopilot? _____

_____

_____

Let's try not to forget that before we could run, we learned how to walk. And, before we mastered walking, we first started by crawling. So, too, should our interactions be shaped with those around us. Not everything in this world comes with an instructional manual, so we have opportunities to create safe spaces to grow and develop when we consider that most of life is really a process of onboarding into the unknown.

Reflection:

_____

_____

_____

_____

_____

_____

_____

_____

_____

_____

_____

_____

_____

_____

_____

_____

_____

_____

_____

_____

_____

_____

_____

WEEK
15

Phone Crisis

Rushing out the door in a hurry is a surefire way to misplace something you need to take with you. The evening I was headed out with a tight deadline was no exception. My phone was missing. My kids attempted to call my phone for me, but I already had a sneaking suspicion that I had turned the ringer off during a previous meeting. Yep. No ringing within earshot of anyone. It was approaching the time when I simply had to leave, so I told my kids that I would be gone for a few hours without it. My daughter became bug-eyed and said, "It will be a crisis if you can't find your phone. How will you go a few hours without it?! I'd *DIE* without my phone." No mystery here that she is a teenager who almost keeps her phone stapled to her body. So, no surprise that not having a phone for a few hours might signal the end of the earth for her.

Eureka! My phone was found on the car floorboard right before leaving to get to my next appointment. I had planned on going to the meeting with or without my phone, and I just happened to get lucky enough to stumble across it. With a huge sense of relief, my daughter told me how happy she was that the lost had been found. I'm certain she was far more excited about it than I was. Tragedy averted in her eyes.

Cellphones are her kryptonite as she quickly loses her resolve and discipline when she hears the ping of friends messaging her. As scientists have confirmed, technology has a strong capacity to make dopamine levels surge in people, hence why they are so magnetic. The cellphone is just one area where a person may experience a stronghold or addictive presence in their life.

After our conversation ended, I thought about how most people have a vice in their life that can create panic if they believe it would be taken away from them. Exercise, work, technology (television, cellphone, laptop), relationships (romantic, family, social), substances (caffeine, alcohol, nicotine), hobbies (sports, shopping, art) are just a few examples of what may rule our lives if we are truly honest with ourselves. While I was amused by my daughter's concern about my "lost" cellphone, I realized that it does have a powerful hold on the lives of many. Just because it isn't my weakness doesn't mean I don't have my own. Upon reflection, I acknowledged that my career-life and fitness pursuits can take center stage, and I would feel a lot like my daughter if these were taken away.

None of these things are inherently good or bad in and of themselves. We give the power to these areas. It is our right and our privilege to pursue the act of disciplined balance in whatever facets we face. It is a gift to get all these first-world bonuses that we often tout as stressors. Instead of labeling or judging them one way or another, make a choice to determine the role they will play in your world. As for my daughter, it may take a while until she can comfortably ignore her social media. For me, it will take a second before I feel great about having a day where I can't find time to squeeze in a planned exercise routine. And that's okay for both of us as we are all works in progress.

Changepoints:

With honest self-reflection, consider the things in your life where you would have an imbalanced level of anxiety if they were taken away:

■ What is it about this activity, object, or person that has caused you to give it power over your life? _____

_____

_____

_____

■ How did this stronghold take center stage in your world? _____

_____

_____

_____

■ What steps can you take to have a healthier approach and balance to it?

_____

_____

_____

_____

■ How will the rest of your life be better served if you create this equilibrium?

_____

_____

_____

_____

■ Who are the accountability partners in your life who can help you address this plan? _____

_____

_____

■ How can you focus on the benefits of creating this balance whereby reducing anxiety? _____

_____

_____

The cellphone will continue to ring and buzz with calls and texts. We can't control that part of the equation. We can, however, decide to put the phone on silent. Just remember that you might end up finding it on the floorboard of your car when you're in a rush. And you'll still survive.

Reflection:

_____

_____

_____

_____

_____

_____

_____

_____

_____

_____

_____

_____

_____

_____

_____

_____

_____

_____

_____

_____

_____

_____

_____

_____

_____

_____

WEEK
16

Fishing Lures

While at work I was telling a story to a coworker about my teenage son sparking a newfound interest in fishing. The coworker then asked me a few questions about my son's passion, trying to determine what he fished for and where he participated in this hobby. I didn't give the friendly conversation a lot of thought as there were business agenda items to cover, so we moved on with the day.

During a break I saw the coworker go to his truck, which is a routine activity for any of the staff. Upon his return, we resumed the meeting. But before official business started, he placed two fishing lures beside me and said he wanted to gift them to my son. He also explained that he assembles and paints fishing lures for his friends, so he wanted my son to experience it for himself.

When I got home, I gave the lures to my son and went about the tasks of the household. Within an hour, I had a text from my son with pictures of himself fishing with the new lures and catching a fish. He also made sure to let me know that custom lures are expensive and very special. His elation at the gesture humbled me. I already knew my coworker was thoughtful, but the feedback from my son revealed the extent of the impact my coworker's kind and generous act made.

This happened because a coworker paid attention to my words and asked insightful questions about my son whom he had never even met. I'll probably never fully appreciate the effect this had on my son being seen, heard, and validated as an individual growing into himself as a young man. If a small fishing lure can change one life, then, imagine what continued generosity and thoughtfulness can do on a larger scale. We should all cast our lines out to pay attention to the details people around us present so we can use them as platforms of encouragement.

Changepoints:

Think of a specific time when you received unexpected kindness because someone was paying attention to your needs:

■ In what ways did this action help you feel validated as a unique individual?

_____
_____
_____

■ What practices do you employ in your personal life to ensure you are in-tune with others? _____

_____
_____
_____

■ How can generosity, awareness, and helpfulness be spread to those in your world who might unknowingly need affirmation? _____

_____
_____
_____

■ How can you be a willing recipient when people try to help or serve you?

_____
_____
_____
_____

■ What does an open spirit do to receiving unexpected acts of thoughtfulness?

_____
_____
_____

■ How do perspectives shift when we seek to validate and appreciate those around us? _____

_____
_____

A three-inch fishing lure ignited a passion in my son. He will remember the gift long after the lure is gone. That's the power of deliberate thoughtfulness.

Reflection:

_____

_____

_____

_____

_____

_____

_____

_____

_____

_____

_____

_____

_____

_____

_____

_____

_____

_____

_____

_____

_____

_____

_____

_____

_____

WEEK
17

Armageddon Pantry

Apocalypse. Armageddon. Doomsday. Call it what you will. When we say these words, images of disasters come to mind, and most of us prefer to be prepared for any looming destruction coming our way. I actually don't devote a great deal of thought to the end of times, so I chuckled when a family member called my basement storage room an "Armageddon Pantry." It is understandable, though, how someone might get that notion given the copious amounts of food staples I keep in my basement.

My "Armageddon Pantry" isn't intended for disaster. The opposite is true, in fact. The pantry is a supply room to enhance the lives of my kids, so when they have hungry bellies, sleepovers with large crowds, or after-school teenage hangouts, there are plenty of options from which they can readily choose. In fact, our guests know we are the place to go for snacks, baked goods, and whatever else they can imagine from the kitchen.

Instead of preparing us for disaster, this pantry serves to prime us for hosting privileges without creating an overt amount of stress. It's one way I have deliberately tried to make my home a place of warmth and welcome for my kids. This stands in stark contrast to the notion of the disaster mindset tied to Armageddon.

Just like many facets of our lives, perspective is crucial for understanding. How we assess our environment is largely based on our lived experience, history, and approach. As such, confusion can occur when we determine something to be truth based on an isolated lens. It's helpful to have conversations surrounding our understanding so we can create dialogue about intent and insight. I was glad to hear my family member discuss this pantry, because it was done from a teasing heart. Furthermore, it provided the platform for me to discuss the real reasons for the development of this food storage, not to mention that it allowed me to invite him to swipe goodies from the snack bin anytime he'd like, to which he readily agreed.

Changepoints:

Ponder elements in your life where context would help someone on the outside better understand your thinking or decision-making:

■ What ways can you proactively inform people of your intent? _____

_____
_____
_____

■ How might you deal with confusion that is created when someone tries to interpret your life without knowing the full spectrum? _____

_____
_____
_____

■ In what ways have you possibly misunderstood the worlds of others? _____

_____
_____
_____

■ How can you best enhance communication whereby increasing the likelihood that people are speaking and listening with the spirit of understanding?

_____
_____
_____
_____

■ What does this open perspective do to help defuse defensiveness?

_____
_____
_____

■ How would you personally benefit from listening to others with the intent of seeking to understand? _____

_____
_____

You may have called my food storage an "Armageddon Pantry." Whatever you decide to label my enormous basement pantry, know that you are invited to partake whether it be a disaster or the true intention of hosting a party. There's enough food for everyone!

Reflection:

_____

_____

_____

_____

_____

_____

_____

_____

_____

_____

_____

_____

_____

_____

_____

_____

_____

_____

_____

_____

_____

_____

_____

WEEK
18

Titles

Upon receiving my doctorate, people would frequently ask me if I would use "Dr. Fleming" as my title. My immediate response was, and still is, "no." I learned quickly that this question would follow: "Why?" I typically explain that I pursued education for my own sake, and I don't want the title to be something isolating me from others. This decision came after my younger brother received his doctoral degree, and he told me that some people don't like doctoral titles because it sends the message that the individual has arrived, and none of us truly arrive if we are self-aware enough to admit it. We are all on a lifelong journey. Upon hearing this, I wholeheartedly agreed and decided to employ the philosophy in my life.

This isn't to say the use of titles is wrong. At times, I find my title is necessary in certain professional and academic settings as a way of designating my capacity in that role. Nonetheless, I currently don't have diplomas hanging on my walls nor do I use my titles unless it is prudent to do so. Official titles can give an air of superiority, separate the individual from others, and serve to hide other facets of our identity. However, we all use titles: mom, friend, faith-based believer, athlete, sister, volunteer, daughter, business-owner, and manager are a few that could be used for me. If I am completely honest with myself, at times I have used these titles to my benefit. For example, I have leaned on my birth-order and title as sister to teach interpersonal communication during workshops. This is a harmless benefit of this designation, but what about the times I might use my title as a mom to dodge other commitments? This isn't outright dishonest, but it might be a strategy for avoiding hurt feelings instead of just declining an invitation. It's easier to create the impression that parenting duties are the reason for not attending a function rather than admitting the event is not where I want to spend my time or energy.

The key is to identify the titles we voluntarily give ourselves, the ones we are born into, and those pinned to us without our explicit permission. For instance, the titles given to me when I was young were "challenging" and "strong-willed." This may be true, but is it accurate because that is who I was from birth or was I nurtured into this role by repeatedly being exposed to those terms?

Once we identify the various titles in our lives, we can then decide what they mean for ourselves personally. The title of "mother" certainly isn't unanimously exemplified throughout the world. The only singular commonality is the physical birth of a child. From there, the definition starts to depart. In Iowa, where I live, "farmer" is another name that can hold a myriad of meanings related to crops, livestock ownership, or management.

Titles can be used for a variety of purposes or ways of categorization, so whether it has a positive or negative impact on an individual largely rests on their internalization of it. How the person uses the designation also reveals their values tied to it. Case in point, my decision not to highlight my doctoral title is something I hold within myself as a compass for how I wish to operate at work. The struggle comes if we hide behind a title for less than admirable reasons, if we are ashamed of a title, or if we don't know why we associate with one.

One title I am unwavering about is "Advocate." I hope eternally this is a piece of my legacy, because it is part of my journey in helping others link to their own beautiful, unique titles.

Changepoints:

Mentally scroll through the various titles you have assumed through your life and pick one to reflect upon:

■ What have you liked or disliked surrounding this title? _____
_____
_____
_____

■ How have you dismissed or hidden behind certain titles to avoid personal accountability? _____
_____
_____
_____

■ In what ways have you possibly misunderstood the titles others use? _____
_____
_____
_____

■ How can you foster new titles in your life, so you continue to grow and develop? _____
_____
_____
_____

■ Are there specific areas you would like to pursue, and why? _____
_____
_____
_____

■ How would you personally benefit from fully identifying, understanding, and aligning with the various titles in your life? _____
_____
_____
_____

Dr. Fleming is an educational threshold I achieved, and it is certainly a part of my identity; however, I'd much rather have my kids' artwork hanging in my office than a framed certificate any day of the week.

Reflection:

_____

_____

_____

_____

_____

_____

_____

_____

_____

_____

_____

_____

_____

_____

_____

_____

_____

_____

_____

_____

_____

_____

_____

_____

_____

WEEK
19

Themes

The phrase, "Don't judge a book by its cover" is essentially asking us to look deeper and figure out the storyline. In other words, what is the theme? We all carry themes with us that shape the way we look at the universe. Some themes are positive, and others aren't so positive. When I went back to school for my doctorate, I began studying perceptions and how they shape decision making. I have wrestled and grappled with this concept for a long time but wasn't able to precisely identify the life-theme creating my pain. I know my strengths and my weaknesses but getting to the heart of internalized "life-themes" is much more difficult because it requires real reflection and processing.

In a dark moment during the summer of my first year in college, a negative theme came to me: not enough. Chronic thoughts flooded my mind. I told myself, "I don't believe I am enough. I don't believe I am enough to be heard, to be seen, and to be loved." Perhaps I had previously avoided the recognition of this theme because I identified it with my dad who had died by suicide when I was a teenager. I have spent most of my life protecting my dad's legacy. In the darkness of that summer moment, I decided that if my dad was gone, I surely must not have been enough for him to stay. I know this isn't logical thinking if you knew my dad, but my 14-year-old-self believed this to some degree and the theme was carrying with me in that present moment. So, my adult-self talked to my adolescent-self and told her she was okay, and fortunately, that dark moment passed.

Thankfully, I don't live in many of those deep, dark moments… but I do carry that "not enough" theme with me in my day-to-day life. For instance, one weekend I ran a race I knew I shouldn't have. And now I'm paying for the aftermath of being significantly injured. I push myself all the time, and often to the betterment of the world around me. I try to work hard and crusade for social causes. I try to be a loyal friend and serve those in need. These are all great things, but what happens when the internal compass is silenced because I am trying to measure myself on the external? I will never be enough if that is my measuring stick, and the cycle of creating and recreating that life theme only continues.

My best friend once asked me if I was "living loved or living to be loved?" Profound. She is encouraging me to shape the ending of my life's book by changing the theme. I can't rewrite past chapters, but I can look at them differently. I can grow from those chapters and decide my own truth, my own theme. I can decide that I will allow who I am to be enough.

Changepoints:

*Assess your life-themes by reflecting
on the following questions:*

■ When do you feel most authentic (positive life-themes) and when do you feel internal tension (disconnected life-themes, which can be positive or negative) and when do you feel angst (negative life-themes)? _____

_____

_____

■ How do the people surrounding you confirm your positive or negative life-themes? _____

_____

_____

■ In what ways are your thoughts driven by your own internal compass or the expectations of others? _____

_____

_____

■ When are you willing to embrace positive life-themes and reframe any negative life-themes you may have? _____

_____

_____

■ Who is going to tell your story and write your desired ending? _____

_____

_____

■ What steps can you take to hold yourself accountable to both identifying your life-themes and putting those you wish to embrace into action? _____

_____

_____

■ What parts of your life will be wonderfully lived if you genuinely accept the life-themes you choose to hold? _____

_____

_____

My theme is now "Enough." In fact, more than enough. This is the new ending for my book that I am always writing.

Reflection:

_____
_____
_____
_____
_____
_____
_____
_____
_____
_____
_____
_____
_____
_____
_____
_____
_____
_____
_____
_____
_____
_____
_____
_____
_____
_____
_____

WEEK
20

Typos

My phone loves to autocorrect the word "people" to "orioles." I'm not sure why my beloved device thinks that humans and a particular bird species are the same thing, but nevertheless, I often inadvertently send comical texts to friends when I'm in a hurry and don't proofread my words. Somehow texting, "Those orioles drive me crazy," doesn't create the same message as, "Those people drive me crazy." And, yes, that is something I've texted my friends, because, yes, some people DO drive me crazy. Orioles might drive me crazy, too, but I can't say I have those regularly flying around my town.

The first obvious takeaway is that I should proofread my writing. I am guilty as charged when it comes to my texting skills; however, the less apparent lesson is the gift of understanding that readers give me when studying my ill-written texts. They try to make sense of my message using context, and then give me grace based on understanding my intent. I think most people who are tech savvy would say they do the same when an incoherent text comes their way.

I wonder how much better our communication would be if we applied the same principles in other interactions with people. Instead of jumping to conclusions, if we took a step back and tried to understand the context of their message and assume good intent, perhaps fewer conflicts, hurt feelings, or misunderstandings would occur. We know that in the world of texting, people are in a hurry and autocorrect goes into hyper drive. Applying the same mindset, when we are busy in the other facets of our lives, maybe it is our less developed brain that kicks into hyper drive, and we speak before reasoning it out. I am sure most of us have been guilty of acting or speaking before thinking. Assuming good intent from others and studying the context of their world – perhaps busyness or stress – would allow us to provide a broader and more compassionate lens on the situation.

If you receive a text from me about some random oriole, please know I'm likely busy with my kids, work, and social life. Birds are lovely creatures, but humans are even lovelier.

Changepoints:

Go through your phone and observe text exchanges where typos exist, and find when grace and understanding is provided among the participants:

■ What makes it easier in texting versus other forms of interactions to provide a more insightful perspective? _____

_____

_____

_____

■ How can we better manifest a "text-forgiving" exchange in other facets of life?

_____

_____

_____

_____

■ In what circumstances do you tend to jump to conclusions or, conversely, provide more compassion? _____

_____

_____

_____

■ How can you help slow down in your own communication with others or when trying to interpret the communication of someone else? _____

_____

_____

_____

■ Are there patterns you can identify to try to address this? _____

_____

_____

_____

■ What outcomes could potentially result? _____

_____

_____

I probably should take some time to study why my phone auto-corrects particular words into peculiar ones, but until then, I wish all my favorite orioles goodness and happy exchanges with one another.

Reflection:

_____

_____

_____

_____

_____

_____

_____

_____

_____

_____

_____

_____

_____

_____

_____

_____

_____

_____

_____

_____

_____

_____

_____

_____

_____

WEEK
21

Vault

We are told from an early age to protect what is valuable. "Put your toy in a safe place so you don't lose it." "Find a special spot, so you don't forget where you placed your wallet." "Make sure you lock up your passport and social security card." People are taught that some things are worth protecting. No one encourages people to give away their driver's license, trust a stranger with their diamond ring, or tweet the passwords to their bank accounts. We don't encourage young children to dismiss their prize stuffed animal or tell a teenager to be reckless with their new brand-named shoes.

Why, then, are we so cavalier with some of the things in life that really matter: our time, our energy, or our relationships? If we would protect these things half as much as we protect our new designer jeans or sports car, we would truly live more fulfilling lives.

One of the hardest things for me to do is to say "no." I must be allergic to the word because I often fail to say "no" to the things that damage my time, energy, and relationships. I am frequently willing to risk myself and those who matter to me for the simple fear of what others might think if I say "no." My inner voice should be my vault. The quiet chamber where I place that which is sacred to me…my relationships, my children, my identity, my energy, my talents, and my hopes. Instead, I shame my inner peace, my personal integrity, and my inward compass to please the people and things that are less significant to how I want to measure my success in life.

As a new year was approaching, I was reflecting and trying to envision the upcoming year. The word that kept scrolling through my mind was the word "vault." I assumed the repetitive thought meant I should place the sacred things of my world into my heart's vault and insulate what matters to me. When I started to reflect on the word, however, I quickly realized that the word vault has multiple meanings. While a vault is a way of protecting valuables, the word also means to propel oneself. How ironic: if I vault what is sacred, I can vault into my intended life. Protecting results in propelling.

How much further would we go if we edited our life down to the things that really mattered to us? If our choices resulted in feeling a sense of true authenticity for how we spent our time, energy, and relationships. All these things are priceless beyond measure, so what if we started treating them as the precious gems they are? If you were told that your energy was worth a million dollars, would you spend it carelessly? If you were told that your time was the most valuable stock on wall street, would you trade it so quickly? If you were told that your family held their weight in gold, would you pawn them off to the closest dealer? I think not. I hope not.

Changepoints:

The dual use of vaults can create powerful tools when an evaluation occurs:

■ What environments feel uneasy when you say "yes" to something that is counter to who you really are? _____

_____

_____

_____

■ Where do you intuitively know you're not protecting the jewels in your life?

_____

_____

_____

■ How often do you go through a day and don't really know how you spent the time? _____

_____

_____

■ When do you feel loneliness even when you're living a crowded or busy life?

_____

_____

_____

■ In what areas are you spinning your wheels on things that could be better spent propelling yourself elsewhere? _____

_____

_____

■ What or who are the critical components of your life? _____

_____

_____

■ What are you doing to ensure you protect these areas? _____

_____

_____

Now is the time for all of us to VAULT. What do you need to vault? Where do you want to vault? Protect these invaluable treasures in your life so in turn you can propel what truly matters.

Reflection:

WEEK

22

Track

My kids enjoy sports, but I've never heard them jump for joy about running. They don't exult in P.E. assessments when the timed mile is required. So, it was a big surprise when my daughter announced she had registered for track. I'm totally supportive of my kids partaking in extracurricular activities, so I didn't want to dim her enthusiasm for trying this newfound sport. Instead, I waited for her to report back to me after her first practice. Upon asking her how it went, she responded, "Track is the worst. You run sooooo much!" Newsflash, child: Track is ALL about running.

I asked her if she was going to continue with the season, and she promptly let me know that track – despite the miserable running – was entirely worth it, because it allows her to be with her friends. She also let me know she doesn't quit something she has signed up to do. In the same breath, however, she made sure to mention that I could refrain from inviting any family members to watch her compete in meets.

She still doesn't love the sport of track. I admire her tenacity though. I also appreciate that she looks for the positives to offset any negatives. When she complains of aches and sore muscles, she still says it is worth it to surround herself with best friends. What a way to keep an eye on the prize!

Similarly, sometimes we find ourselves in situations where we are tackling something that might not rise to the top of our favorite list. This is especially challenging when we haven't chosen the path in front of us. My daughter voluntarily signed up for track, but often we are faced with situations thrown our way. Yet, the mindset of positivity and grit my daughter modeled can be one we employ as well. Rarely is there a case where a rainbow can't be found.

You'll still find my child loathing the track field, but at any given meet you'll also see her laughing, giggling, and having fun with her friends between races. To me, regardless of her finish time she's winning at the game of life.

Changepoints:

While my daughter is highly competitive in many realms, during track she takes this pressure off herself. In your life, picture a time where there was a silver-lining to a hard experience:

■ What did you gain through the process of allowing yourself to still experience what could have initially been considered negative? _____

_____

_____

■ How did the tenacity to push through a challenge benefit you personally or professionally? _____

_____

_____

■ What rewards were manifested by changing your mindset about the situation? Who or what provided this motivation? _____

_____

_____

■ Who in your inner circle models the type of perspective that inspires you to pivot when it would be easy to be drawn into negativity? _____

_____

_____

_____

■ How does this attitude impact the lives of those around them? Conversely, how does a downtrodden perspective affect group morale? _____

_____

_____

_____

■ Describe how "your thoughts become reality" applies to yourself personally.

_____

_____

_____

Thankfully, my kids have wonderful friends who enlighten their worlds. They surround themselves with people who encourage their commitment, growth, and positivity. Even if it now means my daughter is participating in a sport she dreads. She's still running.

Reflection:

_____
_____
_____
_____
_____
_____
_____
_____
_____
_____
_____
_____
_____
_____
_____
_____
_____
_____
_____
_____
_____
_____
_____
_____
_____
_____
_____

WEEK
23

Party PREP

Lots of phrases and metaphors are used to describe the unpleasantries of life, especially those surrounding undesirable tasks. While I love my job, there are aspects that don't fill my bucket as much as others. As such, I tend to avoid them until they become necessary, critical, or in the eleventh hour. Some might call this procrastination, avoidance, or laziness. Others would argue it is human nature to dodge the tasks in life we don't enjoy. Shelves of books have been written on the topic in the attempt to help people find motivation in these areas.

A coworker and I were using some of the common metaphors to describe an accounting task I didn't want to engage in, and we decided that the use of negative phrases probably doesn't help our mindset. We understand why some people might find value in these funny quotes, but we were starting to feel that it wasn't helping us to frame positive energy around tasks we already didn't want to do. We began brainstorming, and together we came up with a mantra: PREP for the Party!

She and I both enjoy social engagements, and we know that preparations are necessary to ensure a successful party. People often don't jump up and down with joy at the thought of the prior arrangements required to be a good host, but they complete these steps to enjoy the outcome of the party. We decided that once a dreaded task is done, especially when it helps in the pursuit of other goals, the feeling is often like hosting a well-received social event. The preparation is worth it for the results. Hence, we decided to embrace the mantra: PREP for the Party!

In this case, PREP is an acronym that helps us lay the groundwork as we decide to embark on challenges. The 'P' represents Priorities (Prioritize Goals). The 'R' stands for Resources (Recognize Needs), and the 'E' is for Environment (Evaluate Surroundings). Lastly, 'P' symbolizes Pavement (Pivot, Move). The simple PREP acronym helps us lay the groundwork so we can be more efficient during the times that are necessary but perhaps not desirable.

P: Priorities (Prioritize Goals)
R: Resources (Recognize Needs)
E: Environment (Evaluate Surroundings)
P: Pavement (Pivot, Move)

Party PREP! Engaging in the needed preplanning and actions allows the intended outcome to unfold. Just like a party, it is worth putting in the effort and then celebrating.

Changepoints:

Ponder the areas in your life or specific tasks you tend to avoid:

■ Why do you procrastinate or stall-out in these areas? _____
_____
_____
_____

■ How can the process of using a positive mantra to reframe these tasks help your approach? _____
_____
_____
_____

■ In what ways could you implement the "PREP for the Party" concepts into your habits? _____
_____
_____
_____

■ How can you hold yourself accountable for completing undesirable tasks in a timely and effective manner to help ensure the greatest potential for success? _____
_____
_____
_____

■ What other parts of your life will be impacted by making these changes?
_____
_____
_____

■ What systems can you implement to help yourself track your goals? _____
_____
_____
_____

Anytime you avoid a necessary function, consider why you are doing so and if a "party" might result if you get it done.

Reflection:

_____

_____

_____

_____

_____

_____

_____

_____

_____

_____

_____

_____

_____

_____

_____

_____

_____

_____

_____

_____

_____

_____

_____

_____

_____

_____

_____

_____

WEEK

24

Fifth Street

Upon arriving at a restaurant selected by a friend and me, I received a text from the person asking if we were at the same location. That's when it dawned on us that this restaurant has a facility on the 300 block of Fifth Street in Des Moines, Iowa, and another on the 300 block of Fifth Street in West Des Moines, Iowa. "Nope," I replied. In fact, I was at the West Des Moines diner, and he was at the Des Moines establishment. He graciously agreed to travel my direction, so I had a few moments to process what had happened to create this communication breakdown. What are the odds that a local restaurant would hold such similarities between two of its locations?

I went back to our initial communication and the texts between us said, "Let's meet at the one on Fifth Street." We both assumed the other knew which city we intended to land in. I'm a resident of West Des Moines, and he is a resident of Des Moines, so it makes sense why confusion had crept in. Our lived experience and perspective shaped our individual analysis. They are neighboring communities in the same county with a very short commute from any given point between the two cities, so they are often discussed as though they are one and the same. This works for efficiency purposes, until it doesn't. Neither of us provided clarifying information or asked distinguishing follow-up questions. As a result, we ended up at two different locations bearing the same name with eerily similar addresses.

We both were correct with our interpretations of the texts between us, and yet we weren't where we anticipated: at the same location to dine together. Thankfully, it was a small blunder in the scheme of things. It was a weekend and neither of us was pressed for time, so we adapted and convened at the same restaurant. Consider, however, if the small blunder was a mistyped decimal point that changed the value of something or a misread message where context wasn't understood and feelings were hurt. A molehill can become a mountain when there is a lack of shared understanding. Alignment and execution can easily misfire by the miniscule, so precision and directness help avoid potential confusion.

Changepoints:

Think of an example where the best of intentions still led you down the wrong path:

■ How did the situation feel while you were experiencing it and then later when you identified the misstep? _____

_____

_____

_____

■ How can the process of avoiding assumptions help create more accurate and useful communication both in personal and professional capacities?

_____

_____

_____

■ In what ways would people evaluate the way you present information to others? Would it benefit from adding more details, emotion, or brevity? _____

_____

_____

_____

■ Who are the people in your life who are easy to interact with and why? What ways do you work together to avoid misunderstandings? _____

_____

_____

_____

■ What flows from having these types of relationships? _____

_____

_____

_____

■ How can this be replicated in the ways you engage with others? _____

_____

_____

_____

The next time you turn on your GPS, consider if you are going to the restaurant in the right city. Don't take it for granted that everyone has explained themselves and knows the intended goal. Entering the proper landmark makes a big difference during your navigation.

Reflection:

_____

_____

_____

_____

_____

_____

_____

_____

_____

_____

_____

_____

_____

_____

_____

_____

_____

_____

_____

_____

_____

_____

_____

_____

_____

WEEK
25

Spring Break

Spring break was approaching, and I heard a teenager share how fellow classmates make comparisons about their spring break adventures upon returning to school. As a truancy mediator, I hear a lot about what children experience behind closed doors. Many of these kids struggle with issues surrounding food, transportation, and housing. Going on an international trip is the last thing on their radar until they return to school, and they get asked where they went during their break. Ouch.

We might think comparing ourselves to others is common high school behavior that adults eventually move beyond. But do we? When we stare at social media, watch reality TV, or yearn for the designer outfit our neighbor is wearing, aren't we essentially doing the same thing? And when we flippantly discuss our recently awarded bonus, weekend getaway to Florida, or the new car we purchased, haven't we set up an environment like the teenager who is asked where they went for spring break? It potentially creates a platform of discomfort or comparison for those who weren't part of the experience.

This isn't to say we shouldn't celebrate our victories or join in the celebrations of others. It is important, however, to be mindful when we discuss the highlights of our lives. The sole spotlight on these bright moments can be unintentionally hurtful to others, and disingenuous to ourselves, if we don't balance our approach with reminders of the valleys or even just the ordinary experiences we encounter.

Showcasing our Valentine's Day flowers is fine if we are sensitive to remember that some people don't wish for a single life. Hallmarking our kids' finest hour is great, until we remember that some people can't have children and other people have children with profound issues. Praising the achievement of an advanced degree is wonderful when we are mindful that education is out of reach for many. We can temper these conversations by thinking about the audience with which we are sharing, along with peppering our words with the less glamourous and very real tales about life. Holistic relationships are filled with gray, blurred lines, and a myriad of colors that paint pictures of authenticity.

Changepoints:

When have you felt excluded from an experience, whether material or otherwise:

■ How did it feel to have to address conversations surrounding this experience? How could you strive to ensure this doesn't happen to others when you talk about your highlights? _____

_____

_____

_____

■ When might you inadvertently use words that isolate others because their lived experience is different from your own? How can you develop your empathy in these areas? _____

_____

_____

_____

■ Who do you know who overtly appears to brag about their accomplishments or possessions? What other underlying themes might be going on to explain the need for this behavior? _____

_____

_____

_____

■ How can you balance when you share about the upsides of life while ensuring that the everyday or downsides are also constructively conveyed? _____

_____

_____

■ In what ways might this equilibrium and vulnerability help others around you?

_____

_____

■ How can this help your own perspective as you absorb information given in the world? _____

_____

Go ahead and revel in the positives life affords you while also considering when, how, and why you share this with others. Cherishing it for yourself in the quietness of your own soul might be all the reward you need.

Reflection:

WEEK
26

Photographs

Someone close to me served as a photographer for an event because pictures were requested for a social media site. Throughout the evening, this person took many pictures. In fact, he indicated about 80 pictures were taken with various attendees from the event. People attending who would normally take pictures with their cell phones put their phones away because they saw him navigating the crowd taking photographs.

When it came time to upload the pictures to the social media website, he discovered a setting on the camera had been turned to the wrong spot and every picture was solid black. Not one of the 80 pictures turned out. Yikes. Thankfully, one attendee had taken five pictures on her cellphone prior to the photographer's arrival, so a handful of pictures existed to document the event. It was disappointing for sure, but certainly not catastrophic.

As I reflected upon people's responses to the lack of pictures, I drew some conclusions. First, it is always a good idea to check progress along the way. Had the photographer looked back at the camera roll periodically he might have caught the error. Secondly, it is a good practice to have a back-up plan as people stopped taking pictures when they saw a photographer present (although understandable since it can create confusion when there is more than one person engaged in a task).

My biggest take-away, however, is to question why we are so tethered to pictures and social media to document the modern world. We can rely so heavily on instant feedback, technological connections, and permanently captured moments that we forget the actual living occurs in being at the event. The experience of just being present at the special occasion should suffice. Pictures are great because they help us recall details from the event, but essentially the memories should come from within. This is one reason social media can be a slippery slope to engage in. When we start living through the experiences of others or rely on the highlight reels captured in photos to tell a story, we run the risk that we miss the opportunities presented when we just soak in life as it comes our way.

My event wasn't any less successful or less meaningful because there weren't 80 pictures of it. The five pictures were sufficient to say that many loving people gathered at a special celebration. The rest of the details can be filled in by sharing the memories with one another directly through real conversations and writings.

Changepoints:

When have you noticed a preoccupation with taking pictures instead of living the moment:

■ How would it feel to set the camera or phone down and soak up the memory?

_____

_____

_____

_____

■ How often do you crop or edit pictures to make the photos appear as polished as possible? How does this run the risk of creating a false narrative of the story? In what ways could the same be occurring when you observe pictures of others? _____

_____

_____

_____

_____

■ Who is a good model of engaging in the moment while also allowing themselves permission to document it when appropriate? _____

_____

_____

_____

■ Why is the pressure so great to project an unending river of perfectly edited pictures or highlight-reel stories? _____

_____

_____

■ What does this do for the way you process the world around yourself?

_____

_____

■ How can you actively engage in the world in a different way? _____

_____

_____

Photographs are just one way to become preoccupied instead of being fully present. Set the distraction down and decide to authentically engage.

Reflection:

_____

_____

_____

_____

_____

_____

_____

_____

_____

_____

_____

_____

_____

_____

_____

_____

_____

_____

_____

_____

_____

_____

_____

_____

_____

_____

WEEK
27

Cookie Mystery

My youngest son was competing in a basketball tournament so I thought it would be fun to bring him a celebratory cookie from the grocery store bakery. I found a cookie that seemed to be suitable based on his interests: a green cookie with the number three frosted on it. Because he is a Larry Bird fan, the green color reflective of the Boston Celtics and the number three reflective of #33 for his jersey seemed to make sense. I bought the cookie and went on my way. As I was driving to the game, I started looking at the cookie and decided I was no longer confident that I was looking at the number three frosted on this dessert. I turned the cookie in various directions to study it. I was now certain I was looking at Latin, Greek, or hieroglyphics.

I decided that unless I was giving my son a cookie with a gang symbol on it, I would proceed with giving him the treat. Upon walking into the gym, a fellow parent looked over my shoulder and said, "Interesting that the bakery made a cookie for the Wahlburgers restaurant." I said, "WHAT?!" Then I told her about my inability to read the numeral "3" on the cookie, and she turned the container and the "3" became a "W." It was written in the exact style and color of the Wahlburgers logo. I found it hysterical that I misinterpreted the cookie so significantly, especially since Wahlburgers is a popular restaurant in the area. In fact, Wahlburgers is the restaurant inside the grocery store where I bought the cookie, so the co-marketing technique was brilliant.

The parent's perspective was exactly what I needed to see it correctly. And once I saw what she pointed out, I could hardly see the previous "3" anymore. The "W" was now so apparent it jumped out. How did I miss it before? Because I had basketball on my mind and was trying to find something my son would like, my mind was validating my search. I lost objectivity because of my mindset. Finding something that resonated with my son's love for Larry Bird and the Boston Celtics clouded my view. Yet, the unbiased parent had a fresh perspective and could read the symbol instantly.

It is easy to fix our view on what is confirming or validating our wishes. Doing so, however, doesn't make the interpretation correct nor does it change the message. The "W" isn't a "3" just because I want it to be. This is why using outside resources and checking for bias helps us better navigate potential blind spots. Thankfully, after the basketball tournament my son devoured his cookie without a second thought that his mom had been utterly clueless when she bought it for him.

Changepoints:

Consider a time when you initially misinterpreted something and then later had it corrected:

■ What areas in your life might leave you susceptible to misunderstandings? Who or what can you lean upon to create checks and balances? _____

_____

_____

_____

■ How can you offer varying perspectives to those in your life who might have tunnel vision on a topic? _____

_____

_____

_____

■ When are you most receptive to feedback from others that might help constructively challenge your worldview? _____

_____

_____

_____

■ Who do you know who remains open, flexible, and transparent about the way they try to intake information? _____

_____

_____

_____

■ What can their lives teach you about the pitfalls of becoming too wedded to a particular mindset? _____

_____

_____

■ How can you integrate their approach to the areas you have identified where your perspective might be limiting or hamstringing you? _____

_____

_____

Regardless how delicious it may be, a cookie doesn't become a Boston Celtics/Larry Bird cookie because I will it to be. It's still a Wahlburgers cookie by its design. And how it was intended to be made is exactly how it should be appreciated. Sometimes we just need another perspective to see it correctly.

Reflection:

_____

_____

_____

_____

_____

_____

_____

_____

_____

_____

_____

_____

_____

_____

_____

_____

_____

_____

_____

_____

WEEK
28

Acronyms

The company I work for decided to change banks after being with a particular establishment for years. Because of the length of time with the old bank, little thought had previously been given about what was needed in a new institution. So, after doing research, a local bank was chosen as the new bank. A team met and a plan was formulated about what financial products we needed and how the transition should occur. Accounts were established and a training timeline was determined.

However, during the introductory meeting there were some red flags, signaling that not all the parties were on the same page with a shared understanding. Acronyms were used by the bank employees that didn't make sense to those of us from my company. For example, we were clueless that FSR stood for Financial Service Representative or that CLM stood for Commercial Loan Manager. We attempted to ask clarifying questions, but I think our lack of knowledge and fear of being embarrassed shut down our willingness to ask more probing questions. As a result, we signed up for a set of financial products we believed fit our needs.

Shortly after this process, we received a little machine in the mail from the new bank. It was absolutely foreign to us. But we asked no questions, moved forward with the training regimen, and signed up for our first educational session. It quickly became evident during this training that we had been signed up for a platform far more robust than our needs. Further, the products we had been assigned didn't communicate with the accounting software we utilize. About ten minutes into this meeting, I stopped the session and asked if the bankers could use language other than acronyms and banking phrases. I then asked if they could communicate with us using simple terms. Thankfully, we had a fabulous trainer, and she quickly assessed that we didn't have the products best suited for our needs. She made a pivot and showed us what she believed we should be using. And she was correct. The simpler products met all our needs and communicated with our accounting software. During this exchange she made a reflective comment about the disservice that had been done by using banking acronyms and terminology only the bankers, and not the clients, understood.

It struck me that many of us fall prey to the tendency of using language that isn't as clear, direct, or simple as it could be. In the process, it muddies the communication and leaves the listener feeling unsure. It also puts the burden on the receiver to ask for more information or clearer instructions. Sometimes they may not even know they didn't understand enough of the message to ask for more clarification. It would be much easier if the communicator took the ownership of having his or her words be direct and transparent by using language at the level of the audience. Thankfully, the issue at the bank was quickly resolved and a great relationship exists between the institution and our company. Think of the times, however, where misunderstandings happen that permanently fracture relationships. How many of those experiences could be avoided by clearer and more thoughtful communication? Not making assumptions that everyone has the same perspective, shared understanding, or knowledge is a better platform to hold conversations.

To this day, I still don't know what the gadget does that was sent to us by the bank. And I still don't know all the acronyms and terms the bankers used in our introductory meeting. But the extra do-hickey and unclear abbreviations weren't needed to make our banking experience successful. In fact, we would have been better served with a concise banking plan, because what we initially experienced was confusion. Either end of the spectrum—too much or too little—can muddy things. Symbolically removing the extra do-hickeys or expanding upon the metaphoric acronyms in our own language could serve us all.

Changepoints:

Think of a time when someone used words, phrases, or acronyms you didn't understand:

■ How did it feel to be without a full context or understanding because of the language used by others? What did you do to bridge the gap? _____

_____

_____

_____

■ When might you inadvertently use words that isolate others because there is a lack of shared understanding? How do these experiences hinder relationships?

_____

_____

_____

■ Who do you know who models clear, direct, and concise communication? How does it aid them and those around them? _____

_____

_____

_____

■ What misunderstandings can be avoided when we choose simpler ways of communicating with others, both in personal and professional arenas? _____

_____

_____

_____

■ What ways can you create checks and balances with your words to communicate clearly with others? _____

_____

_____

■ How can you let others know when you don't fully understand what they are trying to say? _____

_____

_____

There is a time and place to use abbreviations, flowery language, and technical words. Make sure you have the right audience and setting lest it become an unneeded communication acronym or do-hickey.

Reflection:

_____

_____

_____

_____

_____

_____

_____

_____

_____

_____

_____

_____

_____

_____

_____

_____

_____

_____

_____

_____

_____

_____

_____

_____

_____

WEEK

29

Brands

Companies spend countless hours and dollars researching what resonates with consumers when designing concepts surrounding a brand. Some of the most iconic brands use symbols and few, if any words, to create their logo. Company logos communicate the essence of the brand. There are brands so universally understood that their name is synonymous with the product. How often do you say Kleenex for a tissue, Tylenol for acetaminophen, or Band-Aid for a bandage? Talk about marketing and branding genius.

The past decade of my professional life has been spent in the agricultural sector. When I entered this career, I knew very little about the brands associated with the industry; however, any lifelong farmer could have identified these in their sleep. Now, I stand among those who know the company tied to bright red and the organization tied to vibrant green. I don't even need to be given the symbol or logo to know which piece of equipment belongs to which brand just by the colors.

On the other hand, many products don't have brands with the

same mental associations. I travel extensively and yet I can't readily describe many of the brands, logos, or even names of the products I routinely use during my trips. Does anyone know the brand of the charging block they use for their cell phone? I don't. I just know it is very useful to me. I am sure there are people, though, who have the same connection with the travel industry that I do with agriculture. Branding is relative to the end-user. Branding is also relative to the focus people place on it. My kids can spout a laundry list of "must-have" brands that teenagers absolutely can *NOT* survive without. I might not know all these brand names, but I do know they cost this mama a pretty penny.

Think about the brands you are willing to spend a bit more money on. Why do you open your wallet for these products as opposed to other products where generics suffice just fine for you? Consumption of brands conveys something about what we value (quality, style, reputation, prestige, peer-pressure, etc). In essence, the people, activities, and material things we surround ourselves with are reflections of our values. Logos and branding are created for products to delineate these values. The same could be said for the way we spend our time and who we spend our time with. Each carries its own "brand." Much like branding, the resources in our world—people, time, things, activities—have a powerful ability to influence us. Just like our favorite company does when they release their next best and newest. Use the same discernment when selecting the influences in your life that are within your control. And be selective, disciplined, and discerning in your own personal brand you showcase to the world. There is only one of you and it is special.

Changepoints:

Study your favorite company, brand, or marketing influence and see how it correlates with the other areas of your life:

■ How do the things in your life reflect your values? How do they complement or compete with your self-brand? _____

_____

_____

_____

■ Who in your life do you admire for genuinely presenting themselves to the world? How do they convey this image—or brand—to those around them?

_____

_____

_____

■ Which influences in your life could be diminished or increased to help you become the fuller version of the brand you want to show? _____

_____

_____

_____

■ How does the freedom that comes with being authentic translate in the various parts of your world? _____

_____

_____

_____

■ What values are important for you to present to yourself and others?

_____

_____

_____

■ How can you minimize messages that run contrary to them? _____

_____

_____

Branding forms a snapshot into the essence tied to the beliefs, mission, and values of the creator. Market yourself carefully and creatively.

Reflection:

_____

_____

_____

_____

_____

_____

_____

_____

_____

_____

_____

_____

_____

_____

_____

_____

_____

_____

_____

_____

_____

_____

_____

_____

_____

_____

_____

WEEK
30

Mirrors

Go to a hotel lobby, entryway of a home, or any space designed to welcome people and you will typically be greeted by a mirror. Presumably it is to allow guests to make an assessment before presenting themselves. People often take a glance and then make adjustments they deem necessary. Conduct a quick experiment and watch people as they pass mirrors: almost inevitably they will pause and do a quick inventory. The power of the mirror lures us in to take a peek.

Ever notice, however, that not all mirrors present a perfect reflection? The comedy of most circus fun houses is the distorted mirror room where the viewer takes on all shapes and sizes. The draw of a mirror is also why people want a full-length mirror in the closet or bedroom. It's why people strategically place lights near mirrors in bathrooms and why housekeepers are tasked with keeping them clean. The mirror provides information, so a bright, clean, full surface is desirable.

The reflective quality of a mirror tells the viewer to pay attention.

Where we place our focus impacts what we process so it is the very reason we should pay attention to the messages we are given. The reflection in the mirror, however, is just one piece of information, so it is as useful as what we do with it. For example, the image in a mirror is only as vibrant as the light surrounding it. Further, its accuracy stems from how clean the mirrored surface is, and the quality of the materials used in the manufacture of the mirror. Mindlessly trusting that a mirror provides an image that is reflected with 100% accuracy can be limiting, and sometimes dangerous. Hence, automobile mirrors have signs on them that say, "Objects are closer than they appear." The convex design is great for field of view but at the cost of making things appear smaller than they are so the brain believes they are farther away. The warning message on the mirror helps prevent accidents caused by a tool that is intended to benefit the driver.

We have mirrors that surround us in all facets of life: work, family, medical, personal, faith, and academic, to name a few. Some mirrors are unavoidable, but the choice to stare at them is ours. The decision to internalize parts or all of the information is our choice as well. Fortunately, the placement of other mirrors is within our control. Select these mirrors wisely. Do they provide reflections, information, and messages that help you see yourself fully, positively, or accurately? Can you make the necessary adjustments in your life when you pass by these mirrors? Better yet, possess your own figurative pocket-mirror you can pull out when you want to self-reflect, as it is one of the best ways to develop an authentic self-construct and self-image. You can design your own mirror.

Changepoints:

Find a mirror you use frequently and assess what is impacting the reflection. Use this experience to ponder:

■ What do you tend to do when reflections, suggestions, or critiques are provided to you? Does your normal response help or hinder your growth?

_____

_____

_____

■ Which mirrors in your life can be placed strategically so the reflections don't become overwhelming, addicting, or paralyzing? _____

_____

_____

_____

■ Who are the people in your life who provide reflections that add value to your life? _____

_____

_____

■ How captive or free are you from the influence that outside reflections in your life have on you? _____

_____

_____

_____

■ How can you manifest an internal gauge about what you wish to internalize or disregard? _____

_____

_____

■ How are you developing your own practice of self-guided reflecting?

_____

_____

_____

Surround yourself with the right light, materials, and placement so the symbolic mirrors in your life create a helpful image.

Reflection:

_____

_____

_____

_____

_____

_____

_____

_____

_____

_____

_____

_____

_____

_____

_____

_____

_____

_____

_____

_____

_____

_____

_____

_____

WEEK
31

Ingredients

People define "cooking" depending on their view of what it should constitute. I follow the notion that taking pre-made products from the grocery store and heating them up isn't cooking. It's simply completing the process started by another source. There isn't anything wrong with this. I just don't connect it with my definition of cooking. As such, there aren't very many pre-made freezer meals at my house. My fridge and freezer are full, but they are loaded with unassembled food. This isn't to say you won't find prepackaged granola bars or fruit snacks in the cupboard for my kids, but as a rule, my kitchen is void of most pre-made products. Call it frugal, controlling, or healthier, but it's the route I take with most food in my household.

This must not be the state of all kitchens, because I heard my daughter talking about how we are an ingredient house. I had stumbled into the conversation midway, so I thought maybe I misunderstood what she was saying. I asked for clarification, and she said, "At some houses I find food already made. For instance, they might have a package of chocolate chip cookies. At our house you will find floor, sugar, and chocolate chips. It's a great thing, because you can decide to make the cookies yourself or in my case, you just eat the chocolate chips. That's why I say we are an ingredient house."

What an interesting observation. Some people might find the inconvenience of having to make your own cookies a burden. Instead, she focused on the advantages that come with having freedom to pick among available ingredients. I probed a bit more and asked what she thought about preassembled products. In that conversation she commented on how the ease and speed provided benefits. Both scenarios prompted a response that was positive and embracing of the upsides of each.

In our personal lives, perhaps we could view our world as having both solo-ingredient and preassembled approaches. Sometimes we need to look for the ingredients that will make the recipe successful. Other times we can decide to embrace the whole package. Maybe there are relationships, projects, or work that would benefit from an ingredient approach where we find the assets that are helpful. Focusing on the positive, individual ingredients can make processes more rewarding, just like the chocolate chip cookie analogy my daughter had mentioned. In other cases, we might be able to embrace the whole totality, knowing that doing so provides its own benefits of fullness, efficiency, and convenience.

Those living with an individual ingredient approach might glean the values and contributions they need from various people within their world, instead of leaning on a single person. Whereas those living with an assembled or pre-made approach might join an established group or organization that operates under a shared philosophy to achieve the values and contributions they seek. Both have their time and place.

There is more than one way to get a cookie into a kitchen. Bake it with individual ingredients or buy it premade. Either way, the reward is enjoying the dessert, especially the chocolate chips.

Changepoints:

Think of the ways in which you or those around you get a meal to the table:

■ What are the upsides of cooking a meal from scratch? What are the upsides of buying a meal already prepared? How does this mindset transfer to other areas in your life? _____
_____
_____

■ What are the downsides of only valuing ingredient-based cooking or only purchasing premade meals? What areas of your life have this narrow view and how can you shift the thinking? _____
_____
_____

■ Who are the people around you who tend to be flexible in accepting the various ways that the world can present itself? _____
_____
_____

■ How do the thoughts tied to meal prep translate to other areas in your life where you can decide to take an ingredient approach in some facets and a whole package approach in others? _____
_____
_____

■ How might you experience more satisfaction or relief and less frustration or discouragement if you avoided using a rigid approach in your relationships or projects? _____
_____
_____

■ How can you embrace this model with your own views regarding yourself and self-acceptance? _____
_____
_____

The act of living is much like getting dinner to our mouths. There is more than one way to get the job done.

Reflection:

_____

_____

_____

_____

_____

_____

_____

_____

_____

_____

_____

_____

_____

_____

_____

_____

_____

_____

_____

_____

_____

_____

_____

_____

_____

_____

_____

_____

WEEK
32

Of Course

This was the first thing I said when my then-husband asked me to marry him years ago. It was such a natural response to a question where I held absolute certainty. I could have answered, "Sure," but instead I shouted, "Of course!"

While I have no regrets about entering into marriage, I am now divorced. My certainty in the response "Of course!" has changed. This often happens as we grow and develop on our individual paths. Having an identified "Of course!" is great. Giving ourselves permission to let it change, however, is equally rewarding.

At the end of this past year, I started strategizing about my goals for the upcoming year. As I pondered questions about what I wanted, I felt like my theme should be "Of course!" In other words, if I commit to something or turn down options throughout the year, either choice needed to be rooted in an "Of course!" response. When I did a little digging about this often-used phrase, I learned it was initially used to describe a natural course, like a river.

When a river follows its natural course, it moves freely the way it is designed to move. When a river is rerouted or dammed, it takes a great deal of man-made effort to keep that artificial construct in place. When we put artificial actions in place, we essentially negate nature. When we allow something to follow its natural design or intended path, it creates a future that is meant to be, or the "Of course!"

My goal is now to create more natural environments for myself through the process of saying "Yes" or "No" with my best "Of course!" response in mind. For me, this has resulted in editing my life in a way that more accurately reflects the season that I am in, and where I want to be headed. It is difficult for me to turn things down because I tend to people-please; however, I am gaining much-needed transparency and authenticity by honoring my "Of course!" *Your* "Of course!" is going to look different from mine, but that is the beauty of nature. No two rivers look the same. Regardless of where you find yourself, I encourage you to assess your journey and what will help you best steer the course that is natural for you.

Changepoints:

Encourage and stretch yourself to find your "Of Course!" by asking:

■ How do you spend your days? Is your time is fulfilling based on what you think is meaningful or what you believe others wish you to do? _____

_____

_____

_____

■ When do you find yourself regretting the times you say "yes" because of a knee-jerk response to please others? _____

_____

_____

■ If someone could wave a magic wand, what activities would you include or remove in your life? _____

_____

_____

■ What thoughts or activities bring a smile to your face and bring your world energy? _____

_____

_____

■ What negative noise—people, activities, or environments—exists in your life that you need to pare back? _____

_____

_____

■ What obstacles are preventing you from honoring your inner voice?

_____

_____

■ What measures can you take to assess your level of authentic living?

_____

_____

Go pursue your "Of Course!" and let the river inside you chart its natural path.

Reflection:

WEEK

33

Iron Sharpens Iron

I don't know much about the processes of making or sharpening knives, so I was fascinated to learn how using metal can sharpen a knife. If you have ever been to a fancy restaurant or watched a cooking channel, you have likely seen a chef slide a knife against a honing rod. This isn't just for show. It literally is a preparation step that makes the knife ready for service. In my research, I found a handful of concepts to describe why this step is done. For example, the knife becomes far more effective and functional. It removes unwanted irregularities and imperfections. It not only sharpens the knife, but it also makes the knife shine. The knife becomes refined by revealing its natural edge.

Deliberately and methodically rubbing two metals against each other with friction can result in an effective tool! Have you ever tried to cut a tomato with a dull knife? No bueno! Often a dull knife is more dangerous than a sharp knife. The phrase "Iron sharpens iron" talks about the intentional removal of roughness, excess, and blemishes to reveal a shiny, exacting, true edge of the blade. We should all want to be described as sharp instead of dull. To become sharp, however, requires a polishing process. Sometimes polishing can be intense. Yet, when focused on the eventual outcome, the buffing process is worthwhile for the brilliant tool that is revealed at the end.

Each one of us is a blade in the making. Therefore, let's surround ourselves with the necessary iron that sharpens iron. Often this means being challenged to become more than we could be on our own. I have a best friend who continually encourages me to better myself, and often this means being told what I don't want to hear or being exposed to things I wouldn't otherwise see. We call ourselves the "Iron Sharpens Iron Besties," because we know we are polishing, grinding, and buffing each other into a sharper, better place. If you've ever owned an expensive knife, you appreciate the honing rod for the attributes it provides to keep that valuable tool sharp and effective. To put time and resources into a costly knife and then allow it to become dull makes no sense.

It is easy to surround ourselves with people, events, or activities that allow us to go through life unchanged and unchallenged. But what about surrounding ourselves with components that stretch us to sharpen our lens on the world? I don't find the honing process easy, but I do know that I want to have iron in my life that helps reveal my authentic edge.

Changepoints:

As you assess if you have any iron sharpening tools in your world, consider the following:

■ Who in your life constructively challenges you? How do you thank them for this contribution to your life? _____

_____

_____

_____

_____

■ Have you ever attended an event, class, or cause that makes you uncomfortable? If so, what did you take away from that experience? _____

_____

_____

_____

_____

■ Who are the other people in your life who you could consider your "safe place" where you can share in confidence? _____

_____

_____

_____

_____

■ What topics that are steeped in opposing viewpoints make you uncomfortable (e.g. religion, politics, finances…)? _____

_____

_____

_____

■ How do you give yourself permission to express how you honestly feel and do you welcome honest feedback from others? _____

_____

_____

_____

To my fellow knives and honing rods, may you sharpen each other as iron sharpens iron!

Reflection:

_____

_____

_____

_____

_____

_____

_____

_____

_____

_____

_____

_____

_____

_____

_____

_____

_____

_____

_____

_____

_____

_____

_____

_____

_____

WEEK
34

Embassies

Twice, in the past year, I had encounters with government embassies. Both experiences challenged my notion about what I previously believed to be stifled entities. One experience was in Athens and the other was in Amsterdam. The necessity for each was due to miscalculations and missteps on my end.

While traveling by train to the Athenian airport to return home, the train stopped. This is no exaggeration. The train stopped, unannounced, for almost an hour. Not speaking the language, I was baffled until two locals who spoke English explained that this happens on occasion. By the time I got to the airport, I was scrambling. I knew I had no time to get through customs. As I was waiting in line, I heard an American family lamenting about the cost of having to reschedule five plane tickets because they hadn't left enough time the day prior for customs and therefore missed their flights. Panic started to creep up within me. I got to the front counter and told the representative about my recent woes on the train. She looked at her watch and then my scheduled departure time. Her facial expression gave away her concern without uttering a word. I looked at her and said, "I know this isn't your fault or your problem, but is there any way you can help me?"

Kindness spread through her face and she said, "It is easier to offer help when someone is nice and asks for it." She typed away on her computer while reviewing my passport. At this point I was unsure what she was doing, but I had decided to be positive regardless of the outcome because she was being so generous with me. I know her job can't be easy when frequent fliers are often cranky at best. As I was contemplating my next step if I missed the only flight out that day to my destination, she handed me a piece of paper. I asked her what it was, and she said, "You are going through the embassy clearance line." Without fully grasping the impact of what she was saying, I thanked her and quickly went to customs. I handed the card to the gatekeeper who then steered me to a line that is essentially vacant, save for a few men wearing sharp suits. I wasn't dressed for the part at all, but everyone gave me the utmost care. Not a single person at the embassy checkpoint treated me with disdain because of my disheveled appearance. I later learned that I received treatment typically given to dignitaries, which is why I caught my flight with minutes to spare.

The next experience with an embassy was also due to a travel woe, a lost passport. For several hours, I thought my passport had been lost in the taxi from the airport to the hotel. I was advised to go to the American consulate as my trip was very short. Thankfully, the consulate was only a short walk away, so I went to the gate unannounced. And on a Friday afternoon when business for the week was wrapping up. A well-executed plan it was not.

The guard behind the gate was a brood of a man and he wasn't cracking a smile upon my arrival. I proceeded to chatter at him nervously about my passport misstep. Pretty soon, he was laughing at my story as I recounted my day to him. He asked when my flight was departing back to America. Sheepishly, I told him it was Monday. He tried to hide his surprise, and I was genuinely getting concerned about what I would do. After all, it's not every day I lose my passport in another country with only a few days to spare. He then paused and said, "I am going to see what I can do for you." I stood outside the gate for what felt like a long period of time and then he returned with a form. He instructed me that I had been granted an appointment on Monday morning to get an emergency passport created if my original passport didn't surface in the meantime. At this point, he was outside the gate because he had to hand me the documents. So, I did what any normal person does with a huge government security guard, and I hugged him. The man who previously hadn't cracked a smile was now grinning from ear to ear, all because of an interaction tied to a request for help.

The embassy in Greece and the consulate in the Netherlands dispelled my preconceived ideas about formal government entities. But more importantly, both agencies showed that goodness can flow with a simple, sincere request for help. Most people are abundantly capable and willing to meet us where we are when we let them into our world.

Changepoints:

Think of a time when you asked for help, and it was bestowed upon you:

■ How did the experience expand your perspective and trust in the value of asking for help? _____

_____

_____

_____

■ What opportunities do you have to provide help to others, especially when you are specifically asked for it? _____

_____

_____

_____

■ What emotional, mental, or physical benefits are tied to giving and receiving help? _____

_____

_____

■ How does the process of engaging in helpfulness create community among the participants? _____

_____

_____

_____

■ What groups exist that you could meaningfully contribute to? _____

_____

_____

_____

■ How can you be open to receiving help that would lighten your load so you can then pay other forms of help forward into the world? _____

_____

_____

Each of us is a living embassy equipped to participate in help-fulness.

Reflection:

_____

_____

_____

_____

_____

_____

_____

_____

_____

_____

_____

_____

_____

_____

_____

_____

_____

_____

_____

_____

_____

_____

_____

_____

_____

_____

_____

WEEK
35

Oil Change

A new auto service company opened near my workplace, so I decided it would be nice to support a local company over the national company I have used in the past. Because my Subaru Outback was now three years old, I didn't feel as compelled to go to the dealer to have regular maintenance completed. So, I decided to give this new company a whirl. I called to make an appointment, and I was greeted by a friendly gentleman who asked what I needed. I told him I needed an oil change. And this is where the conversation got tricky.

"What type of oil change would you like to get?" the kindly mechanic asked me. "Umm…an oil change," I cautiously replied. He cheerfully responded, "Let me help here. Do you want a conventional or synthetic oil change?" A big pause was followed by, "Umm…I didn't know there was a difference, but I would guess I wouldn't want something synthetic, would I? Maybe I should get the real oil change?" Unbeknownst to me, I had assumed the role of comedian because this man started to laugh. And by laugh, I mean gut-laugh.

He truly wasn't being rude at all, he was laughing in delight. After composing himself he said, "Honey, let's take a minute to learn together. If it were my car, I would get synthetic, because it is better in the long run for your car. This is one time where synthetic isn't a bad thing. It'll cost you more, but I believe it is worth the investment."

I proceeded to thank him for graciously helping me through my ignorance. His next words were profound, "You aren't any different than the rest of us. We all didn't know something important at one point in time. That's why we are here to teach each other." Of course, he is correct. For instance, I didn't attain my doctorate and write my dissertation without first learning how to craft a sentence. And there was a time when this mechanic didn't know all the components that make up a car. Yet today he is a master technician, for which I am grateful. I may love the world of wordsmithing, but I'll leave the automobile talents to him.

It would be a kinder world if everyone gave learners the same grace the mechanic gave me. He could have scoffed at my lack of knowledge, but instead he chose to walk alongside and teach me. Perhaps more people would have an openness to trying new things and taking new adventures if there were safety in doing so. We all have areas of expertise where we can gift our knowledge to others. Conversely, we all have areas of lack where we can be recipients of the gift of another's knowledge. Teacher meet Student. Student meet Teacher.

Changepoints:

Consider a skillset, hobby, interest, discipline, knowledge, or path you have been curious to explore:

■ How could you introduce yourself to this uncharted area? _____

_____
_____
_____

■ Who is a trusted expert or friend who could impart their wisdom or provide needed guidance? _____

_____
_____
_____

■ What areas of expertise or giftedness have you been given that you could share with others? How will you go about sharing this with others? _____

_____
_____
_____

■ How does giving and receiving knowledge from others break down barriers tied to fear? _____

_____
_____
_____

■ What would newfound confidence or a newly acquired skillset do for you? For those around you? _____

_____
_____

■ How are you responsible for being a good steward with the gifts and talents you've been given? _____

_____
_____

Sometimes a little decision about motor oil is all a person needs to realize that teaching opportunities are just a vehicle away.

Reflection:

_____
_____
_____
_____
_____
_____
_____
_____
_____
_____
_____
_____
_____
_____
_____
_____
_____
_____
_____
_____
_____
_____
_____
_____
_____
_____
_____

WEEK

36

Fonts

While I am no marketing expert, I am going out on a limb to say there is probably a great deal of study surrounding the use of fonts in advertising materials. Have you ever picked up something to read only to struggle to read the script because of the font selection? Have you noticed how words are italicized, highlighted, and bolded to draw attention to them? Even font size can make a big difference in how the materials are absorbed by the reader.

A recent conversation at my office landed in the world of font selection, and interestingly, we found that some people have strong opinions about fonts they do or don't like. Amazing to me, I learned many people are quite satisfied always typing in the default font. No offense to the creators of Calibri, but I dislike this font, so I'm not sure why anyone would choose this default font voluntarily. On the other hand, I loathe fonts that are so squirrelly they look like hiero-glyphics. Apparently, I firmly rest in the camp of those with judgmen-tal thoughts about fonts. I'm not even apologetic about my stance.

Lots of psychology inventories use common-day associations to help people understand their personality types: colors, animals, and the four elements. What if we did the same with fonts? Open a Word or Google document and it's easy to find an almost unending list of font options. Try writing everyday words like happy, angry, hot, and cold, and then find fonts that match your perception of the word. Then, type your name. Metaphorically consider two font choices: The font that you project to the world and the font that aligns with your internal compass. Maybe they are the same font, or perhaps two different fonts are selected. Are there metaphoric fonts you would prefer to be associated with?

We all make daily choices that market ourselves to the world. The inventory taken about the way we promote ourselves could be analogous to the font choice—style, size, bolding, italicizing—and how we are portraying our "self" message to the world. If it appears the readers in your world understand you, then likely your metaphoric font choice and word selection are working for you. In the moments you feel misunderstood, however, first consider the words chosen. If those words are accurate with your internal compass and you are still misunderstood, think about the ways in which you are conveying the message. Life is full of font choices that can create nuance in the words. If life is a document, then font choice is a tool we have been given to shape the meaning within the message.

Changepoints:

Open a writing software like Word or Google and type a simple message about yourself. Pause and consider:

■ What types of messages do you tell yourself about who you are that are untrue? Where do you have a harsh view of yourself or an overinflated perspective?

_____

_____

_____

_____

■ How do these messages get conveyed to those around you? _____

_____

_____

_____

_____

■ How can you challenge your false self-concepts so you begin to align your personality font with your truer internal identity? _____

_____

_____

_____

■ Who are the people in your life who you identify as being authentic?

_____

_____

_____

■ How does their authenticity benefit you and those around them? _____

_____

_____

_____

■ How can you assimilate these traits into your own practice? _____

_____

_____

_____

Selecting a font on a computer is an act of aligning the tone with intention, and it is a good theory to utilize in our own lives. Before we write our story, we should consider how we want the message to resonate with our audience.

Reflection:

_____

_____

_____

_____

_____

_____

_____

_____

_____

_____

_____

_____

_____

_____

_____

_____

_____

_____

_____

_____

_____

_____

_____

_____

WEEK
37

License Plates

I'm not a car person, so my knowledge in this area is slim. Yet somehow, I landed myself in a strange new curiosity surrounding license plates. My coworker recently purchased a car and decided to get the new "vanity" plates available in Iowa. Considering there are 25 types of license plates found in Iowa it's pretty amazing that one license plate has risen to the standard of "vanity." It's understandable, though, given that these plates are cool. They are all black with stark white lettering, and they make a statement.

These license plates are so sweet that my son and I created a game about them. We call it, "Is your car cool enough?" Here's the premise: If we see a car donning these all-black plates, we ask ourselves if the car merits such a swanky license plate. On a scale of 0 to 10 we rate the driver's decision to purchase a vanity plate given the car they drive. The game is a lot of fun when you have endless miles of road in front of you.

During the time when we created this game, my son was struggling with something in his life, and I was trying to get him to focus on areas other than this challenge. He stated that it was all he could see around him. I empathized with his discouragement and offered this analogy: Previously when we drove down the road, we paid no attention to the license plates on cars, but now, we can barely pass a vehicle without trying to note what type of license plate it carries. Did anything change about the cars from then until now? No. Our perspective and focus changed. When we decided to shift our eyes to something specific, we created newfound energy. The world around us now felt different even though the environment hadn't changed, but our lens towards it had. How we drive down the road of life is our choice to make. When there appear to be traffic jams, road construction, or unaware drivers, consider if the journey might be more enjoyable if you pay attention to the cool license plates around you.

Changepoints:

Next time you are in a vehicle traveling down the road, see what you can notice that you weren't aware of before:

■ How does it change your experience of being in a car when you decide to have a new focus? _____

_____

_____

_____

_____

■ What are the benefits of recognizing the power of perspective during times when you can't control your environment? _____

_____

_____

_____

■ Once you decide to shift your focus, does it feel more natural to do so again in the future? _____

_____

_____

_____

■ Who are the people in your life who can readily identify the metaphoric "attractive black license plates" on the road of life? _____

_____

_____

_____

■ What traits do they model that you could embrace? _____

_____

_____

■ How have their lives benefited from a positive mental mindset? _____

_____

_____

The world is full of cool license plates, and we can choose to look for them. Then the ride can be more enjoyable, despite whatever potholes might appear, when we allow the positive focus to enter the road of life.

Reflection:

_____
_____
_____
_____
_____
_____
_____
_____
_____
_____
_____
_____
_____
_____
_____
_____
_____
_____
_____
_____
_____
_____
_____

WEEK
38

Blazers

Sometimes, during business trips, I get the opportunity to explore communities. Recently, I was fortunate enough to get to see the sights of Charlotte, North Carolina. I was wandering aimlessly because I believe that's where the magic can be found. Charlotte's Uptown District didn't disappoint.

I decided to check out the NBA Hornets' stadium because my youngest son loves basketball. So, I snapped a few pictures of the complex and went on my merry way. I wasn't paying much attention to my surroundings because I was enamored by the cool vibe of the area. In my state of distraction, I didn't notice being suddenly surrounded by a group of very tall, athletic men. Most were wearing clothing emblazoned with the Trail Blazers logo. And yet, this still didn't send any striking messages to me. Instead, I mixed in with the men because, frankly, they were coming out of a restaurant that looked stellar to me. I wasn't interested in the people exiting the restaurant, I just wanted to scope out the cool place. Then, I noticed that people were paying a lot of attention to these gentlemen. I couldn't figure out what all the hubbub was about, and why these guys were wearing clothing with embroidered Trail Blazers logos when we were clearly in Hornets country. I still didn't give it much thought and just went about my business. I smiled and chatted with some of the men because it seemed like the polite thing to do. Then, someone beside me said, "Isn't it awesome that you just connected with Damian Lillard?" I thought, "Ummm – sure," except I didn't know who he was talking about. I had just wanted to be friendly. As I started to pay more attention, I noticed quite a bit of security around, cameras flashing, and a fleet of buses on the street. These gentlemen started walking into the buses, and then I realized I had stumbled upon the NBA's Portland Trail Blazers team leaving their lunch as they were preparing for the game that night against the Hornets.

I decided not to mingle any further and took a few steps back to quietly snap a few photos to show my son who, by the way, was quite disappointed that I didn't request autographs. I explained to him that I didn't ask for their autographs, because they are just people like us. They want to eat their lunch and prepare for work like the rest of us.

We also discussed how it was extremely funny that I didn't initially realize I was surrounded by professional athletes. I think if I had another opportunity to talk to these athletes, they would likely say they appreciated that I wasn't star struck. I treated them like I would any other person on the street, with a smile and quick chatter. It was a comical reminder that sometimes what we need is a dose of normalcy, to feel surrounded by regularity. We need to move under the radar, to not solely be identified by our occupation, and to be allowed the opportunity to enjoy the small moments without interruption.

Professional athlete or not, we all live in the same world. None of us are more or less special because of our career path or popularity. We all have the same needs, like eating lunch and fulfilling the roles we've been given. Some, however, happen to get to ride on chartered buses and eat at fancy restaurants while doing so.

Changepoints:

Think about your celebrity crush and who you would want to run into on the street:

■ Consider how they might appreciate solitude and normalcy in events that you take for granted, like a simple lunch. How can you hold different perspectives about the routines of your life knowing these same things are gifts to others?

_____

_____

_____

■ In what ways can you better appreciate that popularity, power, and status come with their own challenges? _____

_____

_____

■ How can you interject positivity into the lives of others just by offering gestures like a smile and simple words? _____

_____

_____

_____

■ Despite the career, prestige, or rank someone holds, how can you embrace the notion that interactions can be reciprocal, and we all have something to offer? _____

_____

_____

■ How can you demonstrate an appreciation for where you are in life and that this simplicity can be a reprieve for others? _____

_____

_____

■ In what ways can you shift your perspective to an understanding that no assignment in life is altogether good or bad? _____

_____

_____

The next time you see a group of amazing athletes standing in your midst, consider that the very thing you might be offering them is the unintended gift of not asking for their autograph. While asking for autographs is fine, just seeing others as fellow human beings can also be rewarding.

Reflection:

WEEK

39

Pivot

Friday through Tuesday was perfectly planned. Or so I thought. Then, future planning became present reality. Instead, Friday night my daughter got sick, and we ended up in the after-hours clinic. Pivot. Then, Saturday morning my son announced that he preferred to carpool with a friend to a basketball tournament. Pivot. Then, Sunday afternoon my flight got cancelled with no other flight options for the day. Pivot. Then, Monday morning started with nine hours of travel on what was set to be a two-hour flight. Pivot. Then, Tuesday is rearranged to move all the training curriculum from the previous day into the next jammed-pack day. Pivot.

Sound familiar? The best laid plans can require pivoting skills to execute the change properly. It's not always easy to pivot when things appear to get derailed. But usually there is a positive side to pivoting. Friday night my daughter received care from a medical practitioner who also happens to be married to a long-time friend. Connecting with her again made the appointment more enjoyable for my daughter and me. Saturday I was able to take a different route home from the game, which allowed me to pick up a piece of furniture I purchased. My son wouldn't have been elated to do this, so it was great I could accomplish this alone. Sunday's canceled flight meant my sweet dog, Shiloh, got to spend an extra evening and morning with me without needing dog-sitting care. My airport time on Monday was spent working ahead on reports, so I could return from my travels with a sense of accomplishment.

Embracing a bit of flexibility, something previously not in my nature, allowed me to receive gifts I wouldn't have experienced had I not been open to them. The pivot worked in my favor. Typically, it will when we allow it. For example, my mom and her husband recently had a mix-up with international travel arrangements, and the result was getting to spend the night in a beautiful hotel on the Danube River. The email they sent acknowledged their stress about the uncertainty of not knowing where they were going to stay that evening and then ended with the focus of getting to experience an overnight at a place they otherwise would have missed. Again, the pivot worked in favor of the recipient willing to receive its gift. It doesn't mean we have to ignore the reality of the challenges presented, but there remains the opportunity to have an open mindset.

The keyword is *pivot*, which means turning point. We often mentally translate the word to *divot*, which is a dent or cut made in the ground. Instead of feeling stuck or sunk by a circumstance, which is the mindset that a divot can create, try considering if the experience could be providing an opportunity to pivot. That moment could very well be your chance to turn it into something positive. The next time your plans don't unfold as you imagine, and your mind begins telling you that a divot is on its way, ask yourself to reframe and accept the opportunity to experience the gift in the pivot.

Changepoints:

Remember an experience where the unexpected need for change brought you positivity:

■ How does remembering times when you experienced positivity during a change help soften the desire to be cemented to a plan? What are the areas in your life where you get rigid if plans appear to derail? _____

_____

_____

_____

_____

■ What happens when you become so tethered to an expected outcome that you fail to relax and allow opportunities to become flexible? _____

_____

_____

_____

■ How can you encourage your mind to view change as a positive expression from the universe versus seeing it as the world forcing a divot upon you?

_____

_____

_____

■ Who are the people in your life who model the ability to be nimble when life changes unexpectedly? _____

_____

_____

■ In what ways do they demonstrate an openness to change? _____

_____

_____

■ How can you adopt some of their practices to receive the gifts that pivoting through change can offer? _____

_____

_____

Believe the world offers a pivot and not a divot when change comes your way and see if the experience will bring forth gifts for your benefit.

Reflection:

WEEK

40

And Also...

My daughter is the most delightful spirit in my eyes. She is a complicated soul who is creative, intelligent, random, driven, and protective. She has high expectations of the world, and even higher of herself. From school, to volleyball, to her friendships, she wants "big," and she gives even "bigger." Although she is now a teenager, she has been this unique creature since birth. For instance, when she was just seven years old, she already demonstrated her own view on the world. It was a painfully frigid day in Iowa, and people, me included, were complaining about the intense wind. Many children would chime in with their grumbles about the weather, but her response was, "I just think the wind wants to help the snow blow up in the air to catch the sun's rays so it can sparkle." How's that for perspective?! Not only is it a more creative perspective, but it's also a much healthier point of view at that.

Fast forward to today. When my daughter gets amped about something she will start a story and then realize she has more to share. This is when she says, "And also...". Except that the "And also..." is typically repeated a handful of times until the story reaches its crescendo. I've learned that when she says, "And also..." there is a lot more she is going to tell. Recently, I made her toast with peanut butter and chocolate chips on it. She thanked me for the gesture while simultaneously grabbing the chocolate chip container saying, "And also, this is how we do toppings around here." As you can imagine, a mountain of scrumptious chocolate chips now buried the peanut butter toast below.

She is my "And also..." child. She adds and adds and adds. What starts at one spot—whether it is a story she is telling or toast she is eating—ends somewhere far grander than its origination. She sees the potential. She wants you to experience the fullness of the story or the greatness of what goes on top. To her, life is all about the possibility of seeing how many chocolate chips can be added. Wouldn't it be glorious if we all tried to add to whatever circumstances we were given? Instead of seeing the winter day as a battle with the wind, seeing it instead as a gift of helping the snow to glitter? Instead of seeing the meal we are eating as a routine breakfast, seeing it as the platform to add something fun like chocolate chips? If we so choose, life can be "And also..."

Changepoints:

Consider some of the routine parts of your life or areas that seem challenging:

■ How could you approach what seems on the surface as regular life, or areas of struggle, with an "And also…" mindset? _____
_____
_____
_____

■ What facets of your life could you expand upon to see them with greater opportunities for potential? _____
_____
_____

■ Who are the "And also…" people in your world? How can you integrate their influence into your attitude or perspective? If your "And also…" relationships seem limited, how can you grow your exposure to positive individuals?
_____
_____
_____
_____

■ "And also…" people are those who strive for bigger and greater. This means stretching, growing, and attempting more. What does this look like for you?
_____
_____
_____

■ In what areas could you expand or challenge yourself? _____
_____
_____

■ How can you encourage yourself to embrace a growth mindset? _____
_____
_____
_____

When we allow the universe to become more expansive, the opportunities will be unending and will unfold before us. The snow will start glittering in the wind.

Reflection:

WEEK
41

Deposits and Withdrawals

The world of finances has been at the forefront of my mind lately for two reasons: I've been knee-deep in QuickBooks trying to learn facets of the accounting software, and my oldest son opened his first checking account. Both scenarios were eye opening to me. With QuickBooks, I soon discovered that certain pieces of information didn't readily communicate between the bank statement and the accounting software. With my son, I realized my personal checking history was so engrained in my mind I had forgotten what it was like to be a banking novice. In both cases, my perspective blinded me to the end goals. I was so entrenched with *my* understanding of *my* accounting practices that I failed to remember that the bank statement and software don't glean information through a practice of mindreading. And my years of checking account experience didn't work in my favor when I assumed my son automatically knew all aspects of having a personal checking account. When I discovered that he didn't know what "SSN" meant when he was filling out the paperwork ("social security number" for those who despise the routine use of acronyms in the financial world), I realized I needed to take a step back. I was so entrenched with my mindset I was missing a teachable moment.

After explaining that he did indeed have an SSN issued by the government, I decided to educate him quickly about deposits and withdrawals. I told him that some deposits and withdrawals physically happen, while others might occur behind the scenes electronically. The difference between these highly visible and less apparent transactions also helped shed light on my current QuickBooks woes. I needed to remember that both the highly visible and unseen aspects played important functions in the outcome. Thankfully, with QuickBooks and the in-house accounting platform, a new procedure was established and now both sources of information are captured. And with my son, he now understands how to track the various ways in which debits and credits are created in his account.

The lessons for me surrounding these recent financial experiences have been vast. First, I need to try to take a non-assumptive view when I am exploring something. I should also take the same mindset when I am trying to teach. More importantly, I need to remember that not all transactions in life can be readily seen by others, and yet it doesn't make the impact any less. Metaphorically, the behind-the-scenes debits and credits that people experience are very real even if they aren't outwardly demonstrated and many different things can contribute to the credits and deposits we offer people. Sometimes these smaller, quieter, and softer components will add more to their account than anything else could. Conversely, the debits and withdrawals we take from people can leave them with a negative balance. Their emotional, physical, or mental funds might be so depleted that they have insufficient funds. Worse yet, we might not even know this is the unfortunate status they are facing. Therefore, let's use intentionality in how we practice our "depositing and withdrawing." We only have one account we are given in this life, so let's budget wisely.

Changepoints:

Think about the tangible and intangible aspects of life's deposits and withdrawals:

■ Remember a time when you were given much-needed deposits that added to your bucket. Think about the variables surrounding that person or event. How does it feel to recall that positive memory today? _____

_____

_____

_____

■ Recount a specific situation or individual who debited from your account. What is the memory surrounding this? How does it still impact you today?

_____

_____

_____

■ In what ways does your individual perspective shape the way you view the intent and impact of the transactions experienced in life? Could you shift your view about the intention of others to experience the impact differently?

_____

_____

_____

■ How can you purposefully focus on the deposits and credits you give to your world and those who are in it? _____

_____

_____

■ How can you stretch your metaphoric budget to be more generous to others?

_____

_____

■ What specific things can you do to be more mindful of your transactions (interactions) with others? _____

_____

_____

Give generously and receive with a gracious heart that attempts to assume good intentions of the world.

Reflection:

G.O.A.T.

A common acronym used today is GOAT: the **G**reatest **O**f **A**ll **T**ime. Ask any sports fanatic who the GOAT is within the sport they love, and an answer will quickly follow. Talk to people who are passionate about their assessment, and they will provide a myriad of reasons for their choice. Some will argue that it is based upon sheer performance statistics, while others will say it depends on how the team performs in records and championships. Some will state that the well-rounded players are the ones who make the grade, while others judge based on fan following or corporate sponsorships. Regardless of the threshold used, typically there is consensus among followers about the top handful of "GOATs" for a chosen sport. But perform a search for *THE* absolute best athlete and you will not find a resounding consensus for the number one spot from every source contributing an opinion. And opinions are what they are. While there is compelling evidence for the stance people take, there is no perfectly objective formula for stating what makes someone reach

GOAT status. Watch ESPN on any given day and you will hear experts debate the topic with reverence, spirited passion, and competitive dialogue.

If we allow varying perspectives about what makes an athlete the GOAT, why don't we consider doing the same in other areas of life? Let's continue using a sport to make this point. Because basketball is in my DNA, we'll go with something relatable for me to convey. In basketball, someone might be the GOAT of rebounding and not have the same ability to shoot baskets from the perimeter. Does this mean that athlete has less value? Maybe the team would be woefully weak if they didn't have that individual to rebound for them so they could pass the ball out to the players on the key who can score more. Some basketball players can shoot lights-out under pressure, while others have such great defensive hands that opposing teams loathe dribbling in front of them. The point is it takes many types of players, different fundamental strengths, inspiring coaches, and spectators to comprise team sports. Even the best athletes rely on medical personnel behind the scenes to keep them safe and healthy. The GOAT rarely lives in a bubble alone, and the GOAT is frequently measured on their ability to make the team better and work within a larger network. There have been many athletes who are technically superior who don't reach the level of being a GOAT because of their persona, ego, or toxicity.

The next time you feel that you aren't measuring up to the ranks of a GOAT when you are comparing yourself to others, ask yourself what parameters you are assessing them on, and what you bring that sets you apart. There are many markers for greatness and the comparison game is a perfect recipe for making oneself feel inadequate. Take a broader lens and look for the variables woven throughout, like the coaches who elevate others, the subjective measures used to determine value, the overall performance of the team dynamics, and the fans who cheer on the sidelines. Often, the most inspirational GOAT is someone who doesn't stand in isolation and, instead, reaches their pinnacle with gratitude for the support along the way. Watch the interviews of an athlete you are drawn to, and likely there will be a person who recognizes they are part of a larger story. They see the unique contributions provided by those around them, and they recognize that the elements that bring rise to the GOAT exist within all of us. In turn, their strengths don't diminish the gifts within others. THAT is being a GOAT, and this is present within each of us. We arrive as our own GOAT when we honor ourselves independent of marginalizing comparisons.

Changepoints:

Think about an activity you are passionate about and identify a GOAT you would tie to it:

■ What characteristics of this person inspire you? What traits are worthy of replication? _____

_____

_____

_____

■ While you may see this person as a GOAT, can you find ways even they are not perfect? If they are exemplary and yet with flaws, can you allow the same to be true for yourself? _____

_____

_____

_____

■ In what areas do you inaccurately make comparisons or draw conclusions about yourself or others? _____

_____

_____

_____

■ How can you embrace the unique roles you play in this world? _____

_____

_____

_____

■ How will this perspective change your relationship with yourself and with others? _____

_____

_____

■ What can you do to enhance genuine happiness and support for the gifts in others? _____

_____

_____

The measure of greatness and how a self-GOAT is defined starts with you when you live a purposeful, authentic life that honors the wonderful gifts that only you were designed to give the world.

Reflection:

_____

_____

_____

_____

_____

_____

_____

_____

_____

_____

_____

_____

_____

_____

_____

_____

_____

_____

_____

_____

_____

_____

_____

_____

_____

WEEK
43

Leaves

If you are from the Midwest or visit this region throughout the year, you know we are a part of the United States with four true seasons: winter, spring, summer, and fall. Most people around here love the spring and fall seasons best as these months don't present extreme weather like our winter and summer. The beauty of the spring and fall landscapes is unparalleled, along with revered traditions of tulip festivals in May and bonfires in October. Even the air is amazing during these sacred months.

Yet, this very air is what causes allergies for many who live here. Microscopic pollen wages war on people's sinuses during both seasons. Various trees wreak havoc starting in March, then the ragweed sends its powerful blows in September. These very particles, however, are the necessary backbone to creating the transitions between seasons. Eventually this leads to the magnificent plant life demonstrated in the spring and fall. The buds of newly sprouting leaves and the autumn colors of changing leaves remind us that nothing lasts forever. Even the high heat of summer and the frigid temperatures of winter won't leave their mark indefinitely. Spring and fall eventually greet us with their joyfully opened arms.

Such is life. If the temperatures in your life seem uncomfortably high or woefully low, remember that a season of transition, regrowth, and change could be right on the horizon. The next time you have seasonal spring allergies or rake the fallen leaves of autumn, mindfully tell yourself that you are undergoing these because of the splendor that came first. The next time you dread shoveling the snow or paying the utility bill from withering heat, peacefully tell your soul that this weather is preparing the world for great things to follow.

Jump in the pile of Fall's raked leaves. Run through the sprinklers belonging to Summer. Make snow-angels in Winter's solid ground. Pick the daisies given by the fields of Spring. They *all* have something to offer. Embrace the seasons.

Changepoints:

*Determine the times in life you enjoy
and those you prefer to avoid:*

■ Remember a situation that was hard to endure that eventually led to growth opportunities. What outcomes resulted that couldn't have happened if you hadn't experienced the tumultuous time beforehand? _____

_____

_____

_____

_____

■ Think of ways you can welcome the highs and lows you might face. What serves as your gentle reminder that nothing is forever, the good or the bad?

_____

_____

_____

_____

_____

■ How can you personalize your story to include all seasons? _____

_____

_____

_____

_____

■ How will this change your relationship with the various extremes in life?

_____

_____

_____

_____

■ What can you do to remain authentic to yourself during transitions?

_____

_____

_____

_____

There is a gift to be given and received during all periods of change.

Reflection:

_____

_____

_____

_____

_____

_____

_____

_____

_____

_____

_____

_____

_____

_____

_____

_____

_____

_____

_____

_____

_____

_____

_____

_____

_____

_____

_____

WEEK
44

Sum

If a person were to say to you, "I am finding *some* goodness out there," you would likely tell yourself that the person is noticing facets of positivity around them. This would be an edifying thing to hear for certain. But what if you heard, "I am finding *sum* goodness out there,"? Now THAT would be a great message to internalize as it would mean the person is looking for **total** goodness.

While this word play paints a picture with homophones and the complexities of the English language, it still drives home the point that perspective shapes reality. How often could the lens through which we view the world or the amplifier with which we hear the universe impact the information that is taken in? To say, "*Some* goodness or *sum* goodness," makes a big difference. Intent and understanding certainly matter when defining and applying a thought or word. The word "sum" represents the total and entirety, while the word "some" indicates a part of a whole.

We could give more compassion to those around us if we

reframed things to assume different intent than what we might initially imagine or internalize. We could pause for a moment to explore meaning and definitions that might be new to us. It would feel better to live in an environment where open-mindedness is offered to others. I know I've been a chronic offender myself when I jump to conclusions or assume harsh intent based on what I believe without first seeking to understand. It makes for more defensiveness, aggressiveness, sadness, and unhappiness when I try to write the script for someone else. What if I handed them the pen to share their story with me? It would allow me to absorb their perspective on "sum" instead of my view of "some." The world would be a safer place if we tried to see the total of a person instead of just a part of them. Heaven knows I could use this grace and compassion a LOT as I navigate life. I hope you will seek to find sum goodness in your world.

Changepoints:

Reflect on how you typically shape your perspectives and how you define your world:

■ Think of a specific situation where more context or information would have helped you understand those around you better and provided you the perspective like the word *sum*? What open questions could you have asked to explore this more? _____
_____
_____
_____
_____

■ Consider a time when you were misunderstood because the impact of your behaviors or decisions didn't align with your real intent and the outcome was an experience like the word *some*. What would have been helpful to convey your inner truth? _____
_____
_____
_____
_____

■ What metaphoric lens or amplifier can you use to heighten your sensitivity to the positive or holistic world around you? _____
_____
_____
_____

■ How will doing so soften the sharp edges within yourself? _____
_____
_____
_____

■ What relationships might change as a result? _____
_____
_____
_____

Listen and look for the sum total of what is being presented to you, which is often the goodness in the world.

Reflection:

_____

_____

_____

_____

_____

_____

_____

_____

_____

_____

_____

_____

_____

_____

_____

_____

_____

_____

_____

_____

_____

_____

_____

_____

_____

_____

_____

_____

WEEK
45

Returning

I once went on a trip overseas and I was gone for eight days. Packing for the trip was exciting. Traveling on the airplane was exciting. The trip itself was exciting. Then day eight approached. I was ready to be home. In fact, I was now excited about that. What I was NOT excited about was the process of packing and traveling to return home. While I had enjoyed these necessary efforts when I was ready to embark on my adventure abroad, I wasn't so thrilled to repeat them to get home. Packing and flying now didn't seem so wonderful because I wanted to be home.

When we are away and wish to return somewhere, we often must take the initiative to do the things to get us where we want to be. Ironically, some of these steps are the very things that brought excitement toward the beginning of the journey and now seem challenging, like packing the luggage and flying on the plane. We want to get somewhere without doing the necessary preparations or actions along the way. But if the goal is to return to our destination, we need to keep this priority in focus.

This is where I am in my life now. Some might view the past years of my life as a stage of wandering or struggling. I would have agreed at one time; however, I now try to view this stage as a needed journey of exploration. Some parts I will leave right where they are, in the past. On the other hand, I can also see that I simply reached a crossroads where I decided that I wished to return to the core of Kiley. During that summer I went on an overseas pilgrimage as a symbolic act of taking the next step at the fork in the road. That is where I metaphorically started packing my bags and boarding the airplane to return home to myself, to the fuller, more authentic version of myself. I hope you will join me on the journey of returning to your own version of home, which is to return to oneself.

Changepoints:

Evaluate where you wish to return to and think about the following:

■ Have you arrived at the place where you want to be with yourself? If so, what did you do to get here so that you can remind yourself of it if you ever start to wander? If not, where would you like to be? _____

_____

_____

_____

_____

■ What is the symbolic "baggage" you need to remove from your luggage to lighten your load? What are you dreading to do to prepare for your journey? What should you include so you can arrive safely at your destination?

_____

_____

_____

_____

■ What will the process of "traveling" look like to get you where you intend to be? Will it take you home? _____

_____

_____

_____

_____

■ What are the rewards of returning? _____

_____

_____

_____

■ What are the anticipated joys of embarking on the pilgrimage? _____

_____

_____

_____

_____

Welcome to your adventure of returning. It's the journey of returning to your core and your inner self. It's Home.

Reflection:

_____

_____

_____

_____

_____

_____

_____

_____

_____

_____

_____

_____

_____

_____

_____

_____

_____

_____

_____

_____

_____

_____

_____

_____

_____

_____

_____

_____

_____

WEEK
46

Diabetes and the Dance

I met a beautiful young lady who is a committed runner and fitness enthusiast who also deals with the repercussions of Type I Diabetes. As a child, her world was changed by this life-long disease. When I asked her about her journey with diabetes and running, she taught me an important lesson on coping. She told me that when she first wakes up, her body is not yet vulnerable to the full scope of the effects of diabetes, so she runs immediately upon waking. She essentially circumvents her condition and sways it into functioning in a way that allows her to run.

Isn't that amazing? She has learned the power of modification and adaptation to cope with the discord her body would otherwise feel if she ran at a different time of day. What if we became more like this runner and we didn't avoid the tumult, but learned to dance with it and mastered its steps? This woman found a way to accept the disease while not becoming defeated as its prisoner. She dances *with* it. She knows the moves and steps of diabetes and chooses to work with it and not against it. She is creative, because she gets up early and immediately goes from the bed to the road. She is resourceful, because she makes sure she brings glucose-based snacks, like dried fruit, while she is running to ensure she has safeguards if her body does give her problems. She is realistic, because she goes as far as her body allows and then stops when it communicates that she is pushing too hard. She has learned the dance. Dancing with your discord is a far better coping method than fighting against it.

Take the time to think about what your discord is. If you have an overwhelming schedule, you might consider taking measures to incorporate more deliberate parameters defining your routine. If you have children who are not behaving in a positive manner, you might think about different parenting techniques. If you have an addiction, you might ponder the activators that set the behaviors into motion. If you have a fractured relationship with a friend or spouse, you might explore counseling, mediation, or other communication measures. If you have a health condition, you might search for medical interventions and ways to reduce stress. If you have an emotional or mood disorder, you might want to find a psychologist or books on coping mechanisms. The list of possible discords is endless because they are unique to you. Take the time to figure out potential impediments that bar you from being the fullest version of yourself. But don't stop there. Study it to determine the dance that fits in response to be able to function with it.

If you watch a person dance with his or her partner, they fundamentally must understand the nuances of the other person and anticipate the next moves. A well-orchestrated dance prevents tripping and falling. Much like coping with discord, dancing is successful when there is a plan in place, and we aren't merely stepping wherever we want. Isn't that such a fine metaphor for fluidly working with whatever issues come our way? When we positively approach perceived difficulties with the grace of a dancer, we can work the dance floor by covering the stage with refined anticipation that is rooted in a choreographed plan. So dance, baby, dance!

Changepoints:

As you evaluate the personal discord in your own life, whatever that may be, consider these thoughts:

■ In what ways can you truly understand the nature of your discord so you can get to know it as a potential dance partner? _____

_____

_____

_____

■ How have you considered moves to anticipate upcoming challenges that might occur in your life? _____

_____

_____

_____

■ How will you practice your dance steps to ensure a well-prepared routine?

_____

_____

_____

■ In what ways will you be creative, resourceful, and realistic about the issues that might be presented? _____

_____

_____

_____

■ How will you be prepared for the effects that will likely come your way because of discord? _____

_____

_____

■ What type of risk-reward analysis have you conducted to measure potential outcomes of not coming to terms with your individual challenges? _____

_____

_____

_____

Dance with your discord using your own personal routine and style. Use it to create your own personal choreography. Life is the dance stage, so just get out on the floor and dance!

Reflection:

_____

_____

_____

_____

_____

_____

_____

_____

_____

_____

_____

_____

_____

_____

_____

_____

_____

_____

_____

_____

_____

_____

_____

_____

_____

_____

_____

WEEK
47

Safe Place

Have you ever noticed that pets tend to have places they prefer to go to when they are scared? When there is thunder, many dogs will find a refuge to protect themselves. Some small pets like to burrow in their bedding, while cats often repeatedly find the same spot to hide themselves. It is within our protective instincts to find safety when a threat presents itself.

My dog, Shiloh, is my girl and I am her person. We clicked the moment we became a pair, and she knows I will protect her. As such, she rarely leaves my side. Her devotion is almost comical. I think she knows I love her unconditionally. This is crazy, I know, for those who aren't dog people! Strangely enough, I know she loves me the same. When you study the behaviors of dogs, you will notice that they will give signals about whether they trust someone. Their tails, facial expressions, type of barking, and even their fur will change to express their emotions to others. Dogs strongly understand who and what they consider to be their safe place, and they make no apologies for their feelings.

Shouldn't humans be afforded the same right? We all need safe places, but we often dismiss our internal instincts that tell us if someone or something is safe or not. Some people are overly trusting and don't have discernment to maintain healthy boundaries. Other people, like myself, tend to avoid attachments for fear of getting hurt and then struggle to confide in many people. As counterintuitive as it may sound, I believe people need to become more primitive and instinctive with their protective measures. Enlarge the space if you need to trust more and tighten the space if you need closer boundaries. Don't be afraid to listen to your internal voice that is trying to teach you about your authentic wellness checks. Develop safety systems that are not what the world dictates, but rather what you should peacefully adopt as your own person.

Next time you are on a stroll, look at the natural environment around you and take note of how pets and even wild animals interact with their surroundings. There are many messages we can learn from the four-legged creatures that are part of our world. They inherently seem to know when to trust and when to protect, when to relax and when to be guarded, and when to be energized and when to chill. Let's apply their safety instincts to our everyday lives.

Changepoints:

Evaluate your safety points by considering the following:

■ How do you respond when you feel backed into a corner? Do you retreat or react? Are your responses balanced or extreme? _____
_____
_____
_____

■ What framework do you have in place to deal with stressful, traumatic, or trying experiences? Is this found in a person, a coping strategy, or a physical outlet? _____
_____
_____
_____

■ What steps can you take to believe in yourself enough to care about your needs over what you believe the perceptions of others may be? _____
_____
_____
_____

■ If you either hold back too much or you are overly trusting, what tactics will you use to start encouraging yourself to create healthy safety structures?
_____
_____
_____

■ What hurdles exist for listening to your instincts? _____
_____
_____

■ What actions can you take to start authentically finding safety as you define it?
_____
_____
_____

Find your authentic safe place as it intuitively best serves you.

Reflection:

_____

_____

_____

_____

_____

_____

_____

_____

_____

_____

_____

_____

_____

_____

_____

_____

_____

_____

_____

_____

_____

_____

_____

_____

_____

_____

_____

_____

_____

WEEK

48

Raw

There is a trend to push for products to be unaltered and raw. We want our food to be unprocessed with no additives. We want our clothing to be void of synthetic dyes. We want our water bottles to be free of BPA and our cosmetics to have no harsh chemicals. We see the value of that which was intended to be raw. If you doubt this, look at the boom in organic products, farmer's markets, and home-made craft fairs. Do we value the same properties concerning our emotions, perspectives, and values? Do we want to express these in a raw fashion, and do we appreciate it when people treat us in that manner? If we are advocating for a whole, raw, and organic universe, should it perhaps begin from the inside out?

As a recovering perfectionist, getting me to expose my raw core was very rare. Painting a picture of "having it all together all the time for everyone I encountered" was my mantra. I still struggle with this, because it is my protective instinct to lead people to believe that I have my life in order. At one point, however, I was presented with the daunting challenge of deciding to unveil some rawness to my family. This kind of raw was like ripping off a stale bandage on an infected wound. I was scared to pull off the bandage for fear of what was hiding underneath and what my family would think of my raw self.

To my amazement, my family didn't shake salt on the open sore of my raw self. Instead, they provided me with a healing ointment of acceptance, forgiveness, compassion, and love. Once they saw that my raw was woundedness, they understood me better and loved me all the same. Perhaps they loved me even more. A wound can't heal if it festers unattended under an infected bandage. True wounds that are raw need cleansing, fresh air, and a tender touch. I am grateful for the people in my world who have decided that who I am in my rawest state is worth the investment.

If you are seeking to become raw, find an individual with whom you can discuss your desire to be authentic, and then gauge their reaction. If they appear amenable, start with a small area to evaluate their ability to accept and support you. Journal your experiences that cause you to feel vulnerable. Explore how you feel about those experiences and why you might have associated emotions with those experiences. Ask someone who you love to share with you. Being on the receiving end of allowing someone to be raw can create deeper and greater compassion for the process.

There is a cost with the investment in raw. You can't buy organic fruit for the same cost as conventional fruit, but, if you value getting your produce in its raw state, you are willing to make the investment. The same can be said for human emotion—there is a cost. Just like strawberries grown in organic conditions may initially take more upfront work, the resulting harvest can be magnificent. People invest in that labor of love. When we decide to be raw with who we are in the context of our emotions, perspectives, and values, there is a lot of effort that goes into it. The harvest, though, can be plentiful and rewarding. People invest in that labor of love. Raw is real and real is where it is at.

Changepoints:

Buy raw fruits or vegetables from the store, and study how it changes over time:

■ During what instances are you afraid of being judged because of your authentic feelings and perspectives? _____

_____

_____

_____

_____

■ What topics do you avoid that you believe might make yourself vulnerable to others? _____

_____

_____

_____

_____

■ When do you use other emotions—such as humor, avoidance, or anger—to deflect from how you truly feel? _____

_____

_____

_____

_____

■ What circumstances create self-doubt that the people in your life will accept you right where you are, so you shy away from transparency? _____

_____

_____

_____

_____

■ Who are the people whom you should include within your raw circle of safety or people whom you should edit out? _____

_____

_____

_____

Plant yourself in the raw movement, because the resulting harvest is worthwhile.

Reflection:

WEEK
49

Fractures

A fractured pelvis is the enemy of running. This will wipe out a person's running career faster than you can say, "giddy-up partner!" During an October many moons ago, I trained for a marathon and subsequently injured myself. Hobbling on crutches and not running for seven months caused a high degree of frustration and disappointment because I didn't realize an injury like this could occur from a simple running hobby. I quickly discovered during this recovery period that the best way to mend a fracture is to remove what is causing the pressure. What an earthshattering concept! Removing the pressure that causes injury, in my case excessive running, allowed normalcy to return.

When I finally received a medical release to run again, I had lost confidence and was unsure if I wanted to embark on any future running endeavors because removing the pressure of running the way I had meant I wasn't sure how to run now. I met a fellow runner who imparted great wisdom to me. He said, "You will know if you truly enjoy running if you can hit the trails without concern for what your watch says about how fast you go and how far you run." Initially, this seemed counterintuitive because most runners live and breathe by their pace and distance. I eventually understood what he was implying, though. He was letting me know that if I truly enjoyed running, I would be willing to do it for the sheer act of running by removing the self-imposed pressures. The pace and distance would naturally progress as a result of running for the sake of running. In addition, I would be less likely to injure myself because I would be in tune with my body and not focused only on the outcome.

As I pondered this advice, I realized it applies to many decisions in life:

• Would you do your job even if you didn't get paid? If you simply did what you loved, a natural salary should be forthcoming. You would likely enjoy getting to work each morning as you pursued a meaningful career.

• Would you parent your children according to your intuitive values, without concerns about social pressures? If you simply followed your inner parenting voice, then well-rounded children should grow. You would likely enjoy the parenting process more as you groom children according to their individuality.

• Would you RSVP to events based on your innate interests instead of feelings of guilt? If you simply attend events of your liking, natural "yes" and "no" responses to others could occur. You would likely find your schedule less frenzied and overwhelming.

• Would you buy that material object if you weren't concerned about what the Joneses would think? If you simply made purchases based on your needs and wants, many unneeded debts would be avoided. You would likely own possessions that are gratifying and not filling up wasted space.

After my fractures healed, I discovered I do still love to run. In fact, I appreciate it more now than I did before. I am free to experience the run for what it truly should be: fresh air, stress relief, the beauty of nature, my improved health. Sometimes it takes momentum stopping abruptly to gain valuable perspective about whether that activity improves or decreases your quality of life.

If you are feeling a disconnect with a certain aspect of your life, don't wait for an "injury" to force you to stop and reflect. Pause now and ask yourself why you are making the decisions you are. Careers, schedules, parenting, finances, and relationship are better suited when running without a watch.

Changepoints:

*You might wish to diagnose a
life-fracture by asking:*

■ When do you feel certain and resolute about decisions you are making?

_____

_____

_____

_____

_____

■ What circumstances do you find yourself saying "yes" or "no" to based on what you think others want you to do? _____

_____

_____

_____

_____

■ When might your life choices stem from outer motivations instead of inner values? _____

_____

_____

_____

_____

■ In what cases are you focused on an outcome instead of the process?

_____

_____

_____

_____

_____

■ When do you lack joy in activities that should be fulfilling in and of themselves?

_____

_____

_____

_____

Heal your life-fractures. Address the pressure that is causing friction and pain when you are running on life's pavement.

Reflection:

_____
_____
_____
_____
_____
_____
_____
_____
_____
_____
_____
_____
_____
_____
_____
_____
_____
_____
_____
_____
_____
_____
_____
_____
_____
_____
_____
_____

WEEK
50

FOMO

The acronym FOMO, which stands for the "Fear of Missing Out," was coined to describe the technological phenomenon where people experience compulsive tendencies to check or stay engaged in social media, smart phones, and other tech devices for fear of missing out on potential interactions. The trouble, however, is that FOMO creates environments where people miss out on their real life because they become distracted or consumed by a virtual life.

While FOMO is meant to describe the unhealthy dependency people have on technology, I believe that FOMO has oozed into other arenas, namely the business world. I call it FOMO in HR. As a former Human Resources professional, I think a great disservice is being done in the working world. Employees are almost frantically checking emails, texts, and voicemails because they do not want to miss anything or let anyone down. As a result, we have created a work culture where people expect instantaneous responses to messages. Many business practices seem to imply, "You didn't check your text message within five minutes? Who cares that you are on vacation. You didn't listen to your voicemail after business hours? Who cares that your daughter has a piano recital. You didn't go through all your emails over the weekend? Who cares that you have a honey-do list you want to complete with your partner." Or, what about the employee who doesn't look at their computer all day because they are actually *working*? We are so plugged in that we fail to consider this novel concept!

Because of FOMO, we are creating environments where people aren't truly focused on any specific world. It's a symbolic purgatory, perhaps. And I am the worst offender. In a prior career, I was able to work some of my hours from home and some of my hours from the office. The result, however, was that I was mentally "on-call" ALL the time because I was accessible to staff whenever anyone reached out, night or day. Hindsight has shown me that I needed to take responsibility for not establishing healthy boundaries because heaven forbid, someone couldn't reach me during an HR crisis. After all, I am THE *only* person in THE whole entire universe qualified to handle employment issues. I can now see this was an organizational form of narcissism veiled by my projection of being a good employee for my company.

The problem with FOMO is that you condition those around you to believe they will get an immediate response to anything they present to you…because our behaviors validate those expectations. People tend to operate within the framework that is provided to them. Now, my struggle comes when I decide to set my cell phone down for the day. People are stunned when they don't hear back from me right away. Reestablishing my relationship with technology means moving away from the expectations tied to FOMO. Technology is a beautiful tool, but it can also be a dreadful curse. I am learning that in my world, technology and social media will survive a day without me, shockingly! For you, there might be other areas that will be fine if you decide to momentarily set it aside to focus on something else.

FOMO. The fear of missing out. My FOMO now is understanding that if I keep my eyes glued on anything that continually creates a personal distraction, I WILL miss out, but I will miss out on the things in life that really matter.

Changepoints:

FOMO might be identified in personal or working lives if there is an honest assessment:

- Where have you created FOMO because you truly don't know how you want to spend your time? _____
_____
_____
_____

- What are the areas where you don't establish boundaries with people around you? _____
_____
_____
_____

- Where are the weak spots that don't have well-defined goals or passions you are trying to pursue? _____
_____
_____
_____

- When does the fear of not wanting to lose a job, status, or relationship encourage unhealthy FOMO? _____
_____
_____
_____

- How can you re-engage with the real-life relationships in your world?
_____
_____
_____

- What boundaries can you establish for yourself to know when and how to turn off any distractions? _____
_____
_____

Let's start connecting to a way of life that allows us to be meaningfully focused, which then allows balance to occur.

Reflection:

_____

_____

_____

_____

_____

_____

_____

_____

_____

_____

_____

_____

_____

_____

_____

_____

_____

_____

_____

_____

_____

_____

_____

_____

_____

_____

_____

WEEK

51

Air Quotes

Air Quotes are the quirky little gesture we do with two fingers to frame something we are saying when we don't really believe the message we are giving. Sometimes a stranger simply saying, "Don't do that," is all it takes to realize that when you use air quotes to describe yourself, you are essentially minimizing yourself. After all, if you don't believe the message, why would your audience? This became my philosophy upon meeting a wonderfully animated assistant professor at a local university. He loves to encourage, challenge, and refine business owners. And he isn't afraid to tell you not to use air quotes when you speak. Thanks to his prompt to ponder air quotes, my thought pattern and expression of it have changed. Because of meeting this professor, I understand that the use of this gesture dilutes my message. This also applies to metaphoric, philosophical, or mental air quotes.

My dear friend had joined me for this appointment because she had introduced us, and when we exercised in the early morning hours she spoke highly of this professor and the insights he continually provides her as she develops her business model. Intrigued, I asked if I could attend, or rather crash, a morning coffee with them. Within five minutes of meeting the professor, I knew my time would not be wasted. Early in our conversation he asked me about myself, and I answered by basically giving him a verbal rundown of my resume. He took a nanosecond to tell me that regurgitating my resume and using air quotes told him nothing about me. I was shocked! I had to quickly decide if I was going to be insulted or inspired. I decided to be inspired by the candor of this stranger, who unbeknownst to him is now my spirit mentor.

Throughout our conversation, he challenged me to think about the way I define myself. He prompted me to ask myself, "What do I *really* do (or what do I really *want* to do)? Who is my intended audience? What is the value that I *uniquely* offer the world?" As I pondered these questions it became clear that fluffy answers weren't going to hack it with him. He cut to the chase and challenged me to be succinct in defining myself, and then owning the definition in an authentic way. There is a tendency to use air quotes, both literally and figuratively, because:

We don't want to seem overly confident or arrogant.

We don't want to buck the status quo.

We don't truly know what we are about or where we are going.

We don't want to create false expectations or disappoint others.

We don't want to address our fears.

Now as I begin to develop my vision for myself, I have a better understanding of how I need to move forward. At the very least, I will refrain from using air quotes.

Changepoints:

There might be a tendency to hide behind literal and figurative air quotes if an honest reflection occurs:

■ When do you tend to use air quotes because you don't want to project mis-interpreted arrogance or confidence? _____

_____

_____

_____

■ How do you tend to use vague descriptions about yourself because you haven't fully identified with your talent or attribute? _____

_____

_____

_____

■ In what ways are loose definitions of yourself being used to shelter your authentic wishes and dreams? _____

_____

_____

_____

■ How are air quotes being used as a shield to guard from expectations, fears, or disappointments? _____

_____

_____

_____

■ Why might you be using air quotes in your life in subtle or unconscious ways?

_____

_____

_____

■ What person or action could you use to help better define yourself?

_____

_____

_____

Say good-bye to Air Quotes that are minimizing. Instead, say hello to your clear subject line that projects your rightful identity.

Reflection:

WEEK
52

Three Words

During a period of four months, I watched death impact several lives. One individual I didn't know personally, but I knew the parents. Another was a relative of a dear friend. Last was an individual who was part of my formative childhood years. The circumstances surrounding each passing were different, but one thread remained the same: Upon their deaths, mourners sought to convey the essence of their loved ones while these people were living.

We can all relate to wanting others to know about a person's mark when their crossing arrives. Putting language to someone's soul can be complicated. None of us are solely the highlights or lowlights of our life. We are the sum-total of our waking hours. To winnow it down to a short phrase is challenging. But it's what a tombstone or epitaph requires.

My own dad has been gone for over 30 years. One would think I could summarize his life succinctly after all these years, but when I was given an opportunity one summer to purchase a memorial bench on my childhood playground, I struggled with the limitations the plaque allowed. I only had a given amount of space to communicate a message about my dad. After much thought, I ended up with this, "David Fleming—A Noble Hearted Leader." It was brief, but accurate and true.

Given the recent deaths surrounding me and the memorial process for my dad, I thought about how our lives might be shaped if we pre-wrote the epitaphs, or intended messages, for our lives. If you had an allotment of three or four verbs and adjectives to describe the legacy you wished to imprint on the world, what would they be? Mine might say, "Devoted to Language." It could also say, "Advocate for the Unheard." Perhaps it would read, "Complicated Enigma."

In corporate environments, executives are coached on the necessity for brevity when creating mission statements. If employees can't recite it effortlessly, the odds of sustaining the purpose of the statement diminish. A simple sentence can drive home the point. Research a few organizations, and you will see which send a clear message. One of my favorite mission statements is from the TED brand, the Technology, Enterprise, and Design non-profit that now devotes its energy to expanding ideas globally through TED Talks. Here is its mission statement: Spread Ideas. It is brilliantly simple because the powerful two words carry the message of the entire organization. Think about how you want to define your life in the present. Keep the scope to two, three, or four words. The unfortunate part of epitaphs is that they are written after the fact. Organizational mission statements, however, describe the current purpose, which helps propel goals forward. As you think through your personal description, let's end with three words I believe to be true about you: More Than Enough.

Changepoints:

*Visit a cemetery, read an epitaph, or
study a corporate mission statement:*

■ What are the benefits of proactively writing a personal mission statement
versus waiting for a post-life description? _____

_____

_____

_____

■ How does the process of selecting a handful of chosen words create a focus
around purpose and energy? _____

_____

_____

_____

■ What will you manifest when your eyes are focused on the core of what you
wish your legacy to be? _____

_____

_____

_____

■ How will your time on earth be better aligned with your values if you determine the way you wish to pre-write your story? _____

_____

_____

_____

■ How does your lens affect which positives and negatives enter in? _____

_____

_____

_____

■ In what ways can you align your actions with your beliefs about yourself?

_____

_____

_____

The concern about post-world accounting is that it is timebound. The beauty of present-day messaging is that it is flexible, expandable, and transformable. Choose your mission statment wisely.

Reflection:

_____

_____

_____

_____

_____

_____

_____

_____

_____

_____

_____

_____

_____

_____

_____

_____

_____

_____

_____

_____

_____

_____

_____

_____

_____

_____

_____

Conclusion

As we began this journey, I indicated that these stories are from my own lived experiences, and they are intended to help model the process of capturing imagery to create language and understanding about the internal components of our being. Often these inner constructs are hard to articulate in concrete ways because of the subjective and complicated nature of our psyche, so identifying imagery that resonates with our inner core can help bridge these internal workings with our outer expressions. In doing so, we create avenues to better articulate our values, identity, and purpose, which in turn can buoy our intrapersonal and interpersonal dynamics.

Now is when I pass the pen for you to scribe your own imagery expressions that demonstrate your internal dynamics. Consider the facets of your past that speak to you. Reflect on the areas of your life that are interesting, enjoyable, perplexing, or challenging to you. Think about your greatest accomplishments and your hardest moments. Examine your hobbies, careers, relationships, and interests to see what draws you in and what repels you. Study these mental stories to determine what they are trying to share with you. Find the common threads and areas of departure to decide what they say about your existence. Open-mindedly let the information wash over you so that you expose the spirit you wish to share with the world. That becomes the manifestation of your unique identity.